CLAN BAND

©2021 Michael C. Hubbard.. All rights reserved. No part of this publication may be reproduced or used in any form or by any means, graphic, electronic or mechanical, including photocopying, recording, taping, or information and retrieval systems without written permission of the publisher.

Published by Hellgate Press
(An imprint of L&R Publishing, LLC)
Hellgate Press
PO Box 3531
Ashland, OR 97520
email: sales@hellgatepress.com

Interior & Cover Design: L. Redding

ISBN: 978-1-945163-07-2

Printed and bound in the United States of America
First edition 10 9 8 7 6 5 4 3 2 1

CLAN BAND

A Century of Piping, Drumming, Characters, and Stories from Clan Macleay Pipe Band

MICHAEL C. HUBBARD

Hellgate Press   Ashland, Oregon

This work is dedicated to the late E. Joseph Hewitt III, artist, historian, husband, father, Drum Sergeant, instructor, and good friend to us all. We will never forget you, Joe.

CONTENTS

Preface ix
Introduction 1

PART ONE: HISTORY

    History of Pipes and Drums 7

    Formation of Clan Macleay Pipe Band 11

    Additional Clan Band History 18

    Review and Theories of the Clan Band's Formation
        and History 24

PART TWO: OVERVIEW OF THE CLAN BAND

    What is the Clan Band 29

    By-Laws, Members, Structure and Officers 31

    The Band's Look and Uniforms 36

    Competition...43

    Support and Promotion of Scottish/Celtic Culture
        and Other Entities 46

    Performances 49

    Tunes, Practices and Rehearsals 56

    Instruments 58

    Gunderson/Greenbrier 61

PART THREE: "CLANECDOTES" (STORIES & ANECDOTES) 63

PART FOUR: PHOTOGRAPHS, MUSIC AND MISCELLANEOUS ...97

Acknowledgments 125

About the Author 127

CLAN BAND

PREFACE

I HAVE BEEN PART of the Clan Macleay Pipe Band—known to most as simply the "Clan Band"—based in Portland, Oregon, USA, for forty years—slightly more than one third the existence of such a historical and long-lived organization; yet not as long as a few other current members. Through the years—and admittedly as a product of my own procrastination—I now regret not starting this while we had more former members still with us, or at least with their memories written down...though, as you'll see, there are, fortunately, a few.

While we do have a Band Historian who, along with others in the community, has kept scrapbooks and other material, I have yet to encounter any work more narrative in nature of this bagpipe band. The sad thing is that those from the early days of the band, as well as many from even the 1950s and 1960s, are now gone. Yet rather than mourn what we've lost, we're assembling what we can at this point, perhaps as some sense of celebration of over a century of the Clan Band's continuous existence. And few bands can claim that continuous longevity.

The Northwest, including the U.S. states of Oregon, Washington, and Idaho, and Canadian provinces, such as British Columbia, Alberta and surrounding areas, has been rich with bagpipe bands. In the Portland, Oregon and Vancouver, Washington area (across the Columbia River from each other), so many pipe bands have come and gone. And while a number exist today—whether new ones, or recreations of former bands—the Clan Band has continued...sometimes just plugging along, surviving; sometimes experiencing wonderful growth and heights. It seems only right that a band of this continuously existing history deserves some level of its story told and preserved. Angus Ironside, son of the owners of the once popular The Scottish Shopper, once said, "The Clan Macleay Pipe Band is one of the most successful bands in the country." Whether true or not, the band certainly has endured.

Regardless of that validation, the band is a product, as well as a reflection, of the history of bagpipe bands. The band has been perceived and described with a variety of adjectives and labels through the decades. Some perspectives have been more pejorative (e.g., "geezer band"); but most have considered the band an institution, or the quintessential presence for performance, especially in look (though the band strives for respectable sound, too). No matter the perspective, the band exists still; and we pray that it continues to be a presence.

INTRODUCTION

While this is a story of The Clan Macleay Pipe Band, the "Clan Band," it is only a part and descriptor of a larger narrative, reflecting the experiences of a culture, expressed in many ways beyond bagpipes and drums.

CONNECTIONS

I have a favorite photograph of our band. It's not a studio or other formal shot; it's actually quite casual. It's an outdoor photo of the band after a parade. In looking over the members in the photo, I note that most are now gone. A third of them are gone from this earth; all the rest are either with other bands or no longer playing. In fact, there are only two of us in the photo still actively playing with the band. But it's still my favorite photo; and I'm not certain why.

Perhaps it's the smiles on everyone's face. Perhaps there's a nearly palpable relief in the expressions that we're in a shaded area after finishing a warm parade. Or maybe I'm looking on the faces of those friends we and this planet have lost; and looking fondly and with respect on those who've gone to other piping and drumming pastures, or have just come to the end of their playing days. While I believe all those reasons to be true, there's also a personal connection to that setting of which I was unaware until a year after the photo was taken.

The photo was taken in 1987 in Gladstone Park, following a parade in Gladstone, Oregon, not far from Portland. We are in what's often referred to as "civilian" uniforms, with Prince Charlie coats, hose, ghillie brogues, glens, and so forth. Three drummers are kneeling and smiling broadly in front with the bass drum proudly showing "Clan Macleay Pipe Band" around a rampant lion and St. Andrew's Cross logo. The term "Band of Brothers" could well fit, for only men were in the band back then (today, though, it would be a "Band of Brothers and Sisters").

A year after this band photo, I was sent a family photo by a cousin. It shows some elderly men, shouldering muskets and marching. Amongst the gentlemen in the photo is my great great grandfather, David McArthur, a Scottish immigrant, U.S. Civil War veteran, and eventual homesteader in Oregon. In the photo, he is carrying the U.S. flag. These are Civil War veterans, and the handwritten inscription says, "G.A.R. Drill Gladstone Park July 4, 1914." (G.A.R. is Grand Army of the Republic, referring to the Union Army in that war).

Unknowingly at the time, my bandmates and I were standing for our photograph in roughly the same spot in which my ancestor and his own band of brothers were marching seventy-three years before. The connection was awe-inspiring. And yet there was another connection with our pipe band.

At the time of these Civil War vets' drill, the Clan Band existed. I don't know if there was a Gladstone Parade in 1914 or if the band participated. But it had participated in many parades and other events since its inception; and by doing so, it's connected hundreds of communities and thousands of individuals, no matter their ethnic or cultural backgrounds

Gladstone Park, Gladstone, Oregon, 4 July 1987. Front Row (*l to r*): Ron Galloway, David Day, Joe Hewitt. Second Row (*l to r*): D/M George Paterson, Michael Hubbard, P/M Jeff Brewer, Bill McCulloch, Fraser MacCartney, Bill Cunningham, Howard Cooper. Third Row (*l to r*): Bill Farr, Mark Cameron, David Brown, Don Stewart, John W. Osburn.

The GAR Veterans marching in the same park on 4 July 1914.

COMMUNITY

A friend made a comment of which I've heard variations for many years: "I remember seeing Clan Macleay when I was four years old." But she added another interesting statement: "Think of all the communities you have united in some way through your performances." I had not thought of it put that way.

While people may not share the same religious or political views, or musical tastes, one thread involves what I've heard hundreds of times having to do with individuals who have watched our band in parades and other performances. It's a common thread, including statements such as, "I watched the band every year in the Rose Parade." "My ancestors were from Scotland." "Seeing the band is what made me take up the pipes" [or drums]." "Hearing the bagpipes brings up such emotions in me," and so forth.

Of course, these connections or common links are certainly not unique to the Clan Band. Every pipe band and its members have likely had the same impact and heard the same comments. The only unique aspect is that the Clan Band has experienced this, and made its presence known, for as long as it has.

The communities constitute part of a network, spreading out in space…and even in time. Instructors may have students who spread their knowledge to future generations of musicians, including pipers and drummers. Others may have been inspired by seeing a pipe band, and then learned, joined, or perhaps started other bands, ensuring future ones. Likewise, those of us who play, whether solo or in a band, can relate backward in time to those who preceded us, whether ancestors, instructors, or others. We certainly honor past pipers, drummers, dancers, athletes, and others as we don our kilts and other regalia and play instruments that have been around for a long time.

To add some perspective, perhaps there is another "C": *Continuity*. When we're putting on our uniforms, gathering up our instruments, and performing at some event, nearly all that we do is hardly removed or indistinguishable from what our band members did nearly 120 years ago.

As for bands, those concepts of connections, community, and even continuity apply. Some, like immigrants, played as a continuation of something they did by either starting or joining bands. Others decided to learn, whether as a tribute to their heritage, to connect, or simply because they had always wanted to learn to play. Bands spring from others, and they come and go. Some are fleeting; and some, like the Clan Band, become an institution. Yet they're all related to the history of piping and drumming, particularly when those instruments eventually come together to form bands. For, as will be seen in this narrative, while both instruments existed centuries ago, it was not really that long ago when they were combined to form bands.

CLAN BAND

Part One:
HISTORY

THE HISTORY OF PIPES AND DRUMS

IN 1986, THE LATE Joe Hewitt, former Drum Sergeant of the Clan Band and member of other bands, as well as an artist and historian, wrote an article for the Portland Highland Games program by the title of "1986—The Year of the Pipe Band." While it was primarily a history of pipe bands in the Portland, Oregon, area, it also had an overview of the formation of bands consisting of pipes and drums—generally just referred to as "pipe bands"—including some description of the music, instrumentation and roles of the musicians. Here is a portion of that article [with this author's notes interspersed]:

> *Bagpipes have been around for a long time, the present form of the Great Highland Bagpipe having evolved in the mid-18th century [Joe refers to the Great Highland Bagpipe (GHB) and its origins, although I believe that the GHB, in some form, goes back further. Regardless, pipes with a bag attached in some form go back many centuries and have existed in a wide range of cultures. Even today, there are many versions with their own unique characteristics and sound. The GHB is perhaps the most recognized when the term "bagpipes" is used, and has the chanter*

and three drones: two tenor and one bass]. Early music was generally solo and in the style of Ceol Mor, also known as Piobaireachd ("peebrock").

As Highland regiments became incorporated as part of the regular British army in the late 18th Century, pipers became more institutionalized—even if not officially on the rolls, each company in a battalion nonetheless had at least one. It was in such use, as well as for dances, weddings, and such that Ceol Beag, or the more familiar "light music," of marches, reels, and jigs emerged. Drummers, however, had a much longer association with the military; and unlike pipers, were part of the regimental establishment. Their purpose was also much more involved—they not only tapped cadence, they were also the principal means of transmitting battlefield commands.

Yet it was not until the Crimean War (1854-56), and the years following, that the concept of blending the two instruments really sprouted [The oldest military bands being the Black Watch and the Scots Guards]. Of course, the mixture was not quite as natural as it seems today. Pipe music was changing somewhat to accommodate their military use, and the drumming style was still similar to that of the fife and drums corps.

Drums, in order to compliment [sic] and enhance the pipes, required major style revision to suit the needs of the highly rhythmic 2/4, 3/4, 4/4 and 6/8 marches. This gave rise to innovations in drumming techniques and drum construction, eventually producing one of the most difficult and skillful drumming styles. New drums were developed and/or utilized—the bass drum, the tenor (and alto) drum, and later the rod tensioned side drum (which people often refer to as the "snare"). Thus, the instruments began to evolve mutually and to produce the sound so uniquely associated with pipe bands.

Interrupting here, I'll add that Joe was a drummer, on all the various drums and in many bands, instructor, and Drum Sergeant in the Clan Band for many years, moving on to more competitive pipe bands. So it's understandable that he'd describe the modification and evolution in drums and drumming styles in the creation and trajectory of pipe bands. Although the three-droned GHB was pretty well established by the mid- to late-19th century (and a number of pipers are still playing on such vintage instruments), there have been some changes, too, in pipes.

As will be described in a later section, the basic material—the wood—in constructing bagpipes has changed over time. Although many woods were, and continued to be, used, the most common woods have been some of the densest. Many 19th century sets were made from Cocuswood *(Brya ebenus)* from the Caribbean Islands (e.g., Cuba) and Ebony (often *Diospryros ebenum*, though there are other species). Cocuswood became close to extinction, and African Blackwood (*Dalbergia melanoxylon*) began to dominate in the late 19th, and through the 20th, centuries, although Ebony and other woods are still being used (and African Blackwood is becoming scarcer). In modern times, other materials, including carbon fiber, polyoxymethylene, and other materials are being used.

Sound-wise, tone and tuning has changed, with pitch having risen considerably from the earlier times, which has also affected both the construction and tuning of accompanying drums. Early rope tension drums have given way to mechanical (rods, bolts, etc.) ways to tune, especially given the very tight heads required in this style of drumming. Those heads, too, have changed from skin to synthetic materials.

Returning to Joe's article:

Given their origin, it is quite understandable that the Scottish pipe bands emerged in a military form. There were quite early civilian bands, such as the Govan Police Pipe Band (1860s). But they typically modeled themselves after the military bands, especially since many of the so-called civilian bands were assembled by veterans...

The earliest pipe bands were formed almost exclusively by Scottish or Canadian immigrants [I assume Joe meant those established in the U.S. and other countries], many of whom were pipers from other bands and/or military veterans. In fact, the uniform of the early Portland Scottish Pipe Band was that of the 92nd Gordons, which included surplus Gordon kilts from the Second Boer War (1899-1902).

Consistent with Joe's description, and as will be seen, the Clan Band's origins are tied to a Scottish fraternal society, a chapter of the Order of Scottish Clans, for a number of the early members, including the founders and Pipe Majors, were immigrants. And the band still has Scottish, Canadian, Irish, and other immigrants, as well as members from a variety of ethnic origins.

FORMATION OF CLAN MACLEAY PIPE BAND

As with any history, particularly when a century or more has passed, information consists of memories—sound or not—articles of various types, photographs, notes, and much more. Consequently, there is more than a modicum of mystery and conflicting reports as to the actual date and circumstances of when the Clan Band was first formed. What follows reflects some of that journey to establish the Clan Band's formation date, including some of the individuals and circumstances involved.

When I joined the band, any verbal or written biographies stated that the band was formed in 1927. There is some compelling information in notes written by the now departed Pipe Major Duncan MacKenzie for that date. Yet, as will be seen, there is also information indicating that the band was formed earlier, initially loosely evidenced by photographs from what appear to be earlier dates, showing a bass drum with "Clan Macleay Pipe Band" imprinted on it. A key one, showing a small band with such an inscribed bass drum, has a date of "1912" hand written on the bottom, possibly written by the same Duncan MacKenzie…and dismissed by many as too early. The 1927 date may also have related to when a David Gray took over as Pipe Major; for he was also referred to in a 1931 newspaper article as the band's co-founder. We do know that David Gray played with the Portland Pipe Band (later renamed Portland Scottish), formed in 1906 (although that date, too, is arguable, as some have said 1903).

Some now deceased pipers and drummers reported memories of the Clan Band prior to 1927, yet with nothing of support to those memories. In 2004, the above-referenced Joe Hewitt, posted on the Bob Dunsire site (a popular site for pipers, drummers and others):

> *The Pacific Northwest has a long and rich association with Scottish culture and piping. Pipers are well documented at early trading settlements such at the Hudson's Bay Co. facility at what is now Vancouver WA. The Clan Macleay Pipe Band in Portland, Oregon officially lists the band's beginnings as 'shortly after WW1' and I've often heard the date of 1921 mentioned.*

However, I have seen photographs of the band on parade, which judging from the dress of people and automobiles in the background, I would date from 1914-16. (Part of the problem with trying to tie down the date of formation for the Clan Macleay is that they grew out of a Scottish fraternal order that had origins in the 1800's and often combined forces with The Portland Scottish, another early Portland pipe band.) Regardless of the exact date there is little doubt that the Clan Macleay is one of the oldest pipe bands on the U.S. west coast.

We will look at the two primary sets of references to the band's formation in a moment.

As for the name of the band, what had been reported for generations was that the band was founded originally, and sponsored by, members of the Clan Macleay Fraternal Society (formal name: Clan Macleay, No. 122, Organization of Scottish Clans), an organization formed in 1893 to assist Scottish immigrants moving into the Oregon and Washington area (including, according to one report, helping with obtaining life and disability insurance). [**Note**: The 1893 date is according to an article in *The Oregonian* from 1943, stating that the Clan was celebrating its 50th anniversary, even though an article in The Pipe Band stated 1894]. It was also intended to promote and maintain Scottish culture. Early *Oregonian* articles refer often to that society and events, such as a 26 January 1916 mention of "Burns Anniversary Celebrated," and on 24 January 1920, stating, "Clan Macleay No. 122 Celebrates Anniversary of Robert Burns."

Earlier, in an issue of *The Caledonian*, dated March 1903, mentioned the organization:

Early photo showing a small band with "Clan Macleay Pipe Band" inscribed on the bass drum. The date "1912" is hand written on the bottom.

> Clan Macleay, No. 122, Portland, Ore.,
> Is making its influence felt on the Pacific Coàst, and yet feels in need of a more efficient organ to represent the O.S.C. on the frontier of our land. This clan will be represented at the August convention in Cleveland by the secretary, Alexander G. Brown.

The Macleay name was prominent in Portland and reportedly came first from Donald Macleay, merchant, financier, and philanthropist, born in August, 1834 in Ross-shire, Scotland. He moved from California to Oregon in 1866 and started, with William Corbitt, a grocery, shipping, and commission business called Corbitt & Macleay. Donald was also involved in starting such organizations as The Arlington Club, and donated property (e.g., Macleay Park) and other things to the community. It is reported that The Clan Macleay Lodge No. 122 was named after him…and thus, perhaps indirectly, the Clan Band.

Let us return to the debate—and fact-finding journey—regarding the band's formation date:

1927: The aforementioned Duncan MacKenzie has left us notes that give a seemingly credible account of the band's formation; or perhaps formalization. In one, dated 26 November 1926, he wrote: "Clansman Hugh MacKenzie made a favorable report on the progress of the contemplated Clan MacLeay [sic] Pipe Band." [Note: P/M MacKenzie used a capital "L" in "Macleay" in all his notes]."

Hugh MacKenzie was Duncan's father, and had been admitted to the Lodge No. 122 on 12 March 1926 at age forty-nine. Duncan was admitted on 19 March 1933 at age sixteen. The word "contemplated" in Duncan's note would certainly imply that the band had not yet been formed.

Another note by P/M MacKenzie, dated 27 May 1927, stated: "Financial Sec. read a communication from DOS [Daughters of Scotia] enclosing a check for 25.00 for Clan MacLeay Pipe Band."

Another, on 24 June 1927: "After the initiation, Clan MacLeay Pipe Band played a few selections. The members of the band now are as follows. Clansman D. Gray, E. Dick & J. Brown Pipers, Wm Jeffrey, Base [sic] Drum, J Austin side drum."

On 8 July 1927: "Piper Gray announced he had received a check for 5.00 from P.C. J.P. Stewart towards buying equipment for the Clan MacLeay Pipe Band. Sentinel Hugh MacKenzie on behalf of Clan MacLeay Pipe Band asked for the use of the Redmen Hall (S.E. 9th & Hawthorne) on the 5th Friday of July for marching practice for the Band. Request granted."

There were more notes from 1927 and 1928, mostly having to do with donations and buying equipment (e.g., one from 12 October 1928: "Clansman MacKenzie made motion, the Clan stand expense of Roping big Drum & securing new bag for set of Pipes.") But all point to two figures in David Gray, who played with Portland (Scottish) Pipe Band, and Hugh MacKenzie—the former becoming Pipe Major of Clan Macleay and the latter being Band Manager—approaching the Clan Macleay Lodge No. 122 for sponsorship; perhaps for more.

Earlier Formation Date: A different story of the Clan Band's formation came from the now departed former Pipe Major of Portland Scottish Pipe Band, Harry Fenley. He stated that the Clan Band started from members of Portland Pipe Band as a "split in the band in the early twenties—the start of the Clan Macleay Pipe Band—as having its basis in an ongoing union dispute at the time in which the feeling between the union and non-union members of the band got a little dicey." We do not know to what union he was referring; nor do we know if the members forming the Clan Band were union or non-union.

Not helping matters, a 1957 issue of *The Pipe Band, Official Organ of The Scottish Pipe Band Association*, had an article on the band, outlining the formation of The Clan Macleay No. 122 "back to 1894" and "in years past they had a Clan Band..." The article indicated that the band lost many members during

World War II, and that "the Clan had no official Pipe Band" during that period. Further, it stated that the band was reorganized in 1954 and "...officially adopted by the Clan..." and "...with "Duncan MacKenzie as Pipe-Major and Ronald Miller as Drum-Sergeant." [**Note**: As will be seen later, the Clan Band was, in fact, active during the 1940s and WWII; so we're not certain what "reorganized" meant].

Supporting the earlier-referenced post by Joe Hewitt, in which he felt there was evidence of the band's existence, possibly as early as 1914-16, were several articles from *The Oregonian* and other newspapers.

One of the earliest references to a possible Clan Band is an article from 28 October 1912, regarding "...opening game of the Portland Soccer Football League..." in which was added "...The Clan Macleay band of bagpipes and drums and fifes played selections during the game..." [The reference to "fifes," not a traditional part of pipe bands, is interesting!]. Curiously, an article in *The Morning Oregonian* from the same date had the same quote, yet was referencing a cricket match. Another article in the *Oregon City Enterprise*, with an earlier date of 12 July 1912, stated, "...Many Scottish people of Portland as well as of this city celebrated the Fourth at Canemah Park...one of the most enjoyable celebrations ever held by the Clan Macleay Society. Among the features of the program were dancing, bagpipe selections, sword dancing and races...."

Another article, dated 16 July 1922, regarding some event, stated, "...composed of members of the Daughters of Scotia, Clan Macleay and the kilty band..."

None of the articles unearthed preceding 1926 specifically mentioned "Clan Macleay Pipe Band." And we know that the

Portland Pipe Band performed at some events hosted by the Clan Macleay Lodge. If no specific band was mentioned, with just a statement about the Lodge and something akin to "the bagpipe band," such articles left us with no specific knowledge as to what band was referenced.

However, a breakthrough occurred in an obituary, dated 19 August 1913, in *The Morning Oregonian*, regarding a John Smith, for it also contained a photograph:

> John Smith, a well-known Scotch clansman, died at Good Samaritan Hospital Sunday of typhoid fever after a short illness. He was a native of Scotland, and was 37 years old, had been an active member of Clan Macleay and leader of the bagpipe band. Mr. Smith was also a member of Multnomah Camp No. 72, Woodman of the World, and Mt. Tabor Lodge, A.P. and A.M. A wife and little son survive him. The funeral will be held tomorrow at 2 o'clock...Clan Macleay will supply the pallbearers, dressed in uniform.

Mr. Smith's photograph had him in uniform, and in comparing it to the 1912 photograph, he is seen as the Pipe Major, clearly establishing that the Clan Band existed as early as 1912. Was it formed even earlier? As yet, we do not know.

ADDITIONAL CLAN BAND HISTORY

In the early twentieth century, and around the time of the formation of the Clan Band, we do know that there were at least three bagpipe

John Smith's obituary, 1913

bands in the Portland area. There was also considerable interaction between them. It's apparent that the bands in the Portland, Oregon and Vancouver, Washington area in the early twentieth century shared a lot early on, including players, uniforms, and even bass drums, until each began to establish more autonomy.

As for the earlier referenced Portland (Scottish) Pipe Band, another now departed Pipe Major of that band, Bob Johnson, wrote, "The Portland Pipe Band was formed in 1906 at a tavern at First and Madison [downtown Portland, east of the Willamette River] operated by one of the old pipers, James Moon, and existed until 1977 when it disbanded, having changed its name to Portland Scottish Pipe Band sometime in the 50's." As for the name change, adding "Scottish," it's interesting that *Oregonian* articles as early as 1913 mention "Portland Scottish Pipe Band." Perhaps that was simply an editorial addition in recognizing the band as "Scottish." Bob stated further, "The Canadian Legion Pipe Band, Post #17, was essentially the Portland Pipe Band with a Canadian Legion bass drum head… and the band functioned about the time of and during a Legion Convention in Portland in 1933 or 1934." An article in the 1986 Portland Highland Games program (the earlier-referenced "1986 The Year of the Pipe Band") stated: "Its members were essentially the same in the two bands—they simply changed bass drums, and perhaps uniforms, to play as one or the other, depending upon the event." Other sources indicated that the Canadian Legion band disbanded sometime in the 1940s, although the Portland Games article indicated that it existed into the 1950s.

Regardless of the earlier date the Clan Band was formed, it was active and mentioned by name frequently in newspapers and other media from the late twenties on, especially in the

1930s. Here are just a few snippets from articles over the next couple decades after the 1920s:

> Oregonian *article, dated 24 May 1930:* "British Societies To Get Together" *at which played* "...Piper, David Gray with his Clan Macleay pipe band."

> *20 May 1931:* "British Benevolent Society Will Celebrate Next Saturday...at which...The concert program: Selections Clan Macleay pipe band; director, Piper David Gray."

> *13 Dec 1931:* "An attraction at the game will be the Clan Macleay pipe band of the Order of Scottish Glans. They will be in full kiltie regalia..."

> *17 Nov 1937: [This is a funny editorial making fun of an announcer of an event]:* "That Hawaiian orchestra leader's name ain't Whoopie. It's Hoe-se-pi. Where's the Clan Macleay pipe band nowadays? They ought to broadcast 15 minutes a week just to flush out loudspeakers contaminated with germs from so many programs that are weak and silly."

Regarding the earlier mentioned 1957 article from "The Pipe Band," referring to inactivity during the 1940s, and specifically during WWII, there are several articles from the 1940s indicating that the band, though perhaps small in number, was still active.

> *20 Feb 1941:* "The Macleay pipe band will sponsor a concert and dance for the benefit of the Scottish branch of the British Red Cross Friday at 8 P.M. in Red Men's hall, S.E. 9th avenue and Hawthorne boulevard."

CLAN BAND

The Old Portland Pipe Band, ca. early 1920s. *L to R*: Dave Henderson, Walter Loch, Jim Inglis (bass drummer), unknown, Bill Gray, Howard Austin, Dave Gray.

8 March 1941: Re: "…benefit of British war relief of Oregon…" "…the Clan Macleay bagpipes will play, led by Pipe Major David Gray…"

21 Sept 1943: "Clan to observe 50th Anniversary. Members of Clan Macleay No. 122, Order of Scottish Clans, will celebrate the 50th anniversary of the institution of the clan Saturday night in the Masonic temple, S.W. Park avenue and Main street… Donald Harris Jr., chief of Clan Macleay, will be the only living charter member, John 'Jack' Austin. The Clan Macleay pipe band in highland costumes will play."

29 July 1946: Re: Picnic at Silver Falls State Park. "Clan Macleay, order of Scottish clan, No. 122, of Portland will be present with a pipe band. Other bagpipe players, including well-known W.R. Tomison of Silverton, are expected to attend…"

24 April 1949: "*Portland's two bagpipe bands, the pipers of the Clan Macleay and the City of Portland Bagpipe band (Not to be confused with Portland Pipe Band), got their uniforms from Glasgow before the war. A kilt uniform with all the trimmings cost, prewar prices, a cool hundred, and the pipes are verra [sic] expensive, too—a good set about $100. In a pipe band are eight to ten pipers, four side drummers, a bass and one or two tenor drummers. Leader is the pipe major. Pipe major for both Portland bands is a young man named Capt. Chester A. MacNeill Jr., a merchant marine. Men who play the pipes are practically always of Scottish descent, though many are like Captain MacNeill, American born. The urge to play bagpipes is in the blood. Pipe Major MacNeill has currently five pupils. Neighbors around his Sellwood home, 114 S.E. Tenino avenue, have never made any complaints. As for the pipe major's wife, he played pipes while he was courting, so she knew what she was getting into.*"

28 Feb 1950: "*Sir Harry Louden, beloved little Scottish entertainer, was remembered in Portland Monday by Scottish groups saddened by his death. Charles Cumming, tanist of Clan Macleay, recalled that Sir Harry was met on one of these visits [either 1929 or 1932] by the Clan bagpipe band, which skirled him through the train depot with lusty pipe music, much to the amusement of the entertainer's fellow passengers.*"

27 May 1950: Re: Dedication of a "*brick and marble bench at the Seaside turnaround.*" "*The bench was dedicated by Governor Douglas McKay…Clan Macleay pipe band of Portland piped the music at the ceremony….*"

3 Oct 1954: "Pipers Plan Tartan Ball. Event Scheduled For October 23. A tartan ball is planned October 23 in the Grand ballroom of the Masonic temple by Clan Macleay bagpipe band as a charity and uniform benefit. Members of the band will be assisted by members of White Heather lodge, Daughters of Scotia. Dancing will begin at 8 p.m., with a program of entertainment planned during intermission. In charge of arrangements will be Duncan MacKenzie, Bruce Stewart, David Patterson and Ronald Miller."

Returning to the topic of the bond between the Clan Band and the Clan Macleay Lodge, the two remained related, perhaps on and off, although the band eventually formed its own by-laws and became more autonomous. Still, until as late as the early 1990s, the band continued to play at the Society's Robert Burns Dinners, as well as at their member installation ceremonies.

The dates of the band's formation, who was involved, and so forth were not the only part of the history of the band with conflicting stories. At one point, in addition to the band's name, the bass drum sported, "The Governor's Own." I was told that this was allegedly granted by Governor Tom McCall. However, there is a photograph of the band in 1961 with the following on the bass drum: "The Oregon Governor's Bagpipe Band." McCall was not governor until 1967. Mark Hatfield was governor in 1961. Bonnie Heather Blyth (MacKenzie), married to Colin MacKenzie, and thus Duncan MacKenzie's daughter-in-law, stated that she danced at Mark Hatfield's inauguration, and stated further that it was, in fact, Governor Hatfield who named the band "The Governor's." That is the most credible account; and I certainly recall talking with the then retired Senator Hatfield who was very appreciative of the band whenever he was in attendance at any performance.

Whether the Clan Band was formed independently or, as reported, sprang from Portland Pipe Band, it has been the only survivor of those early pipe bands in the Portland and surrounding area. Many others have come and gone, and a number exist today; but none with the history (yet) of the Clan Band.

REVIEW AND THEORIES OF THE CLAN BAND'S FORMATION AND HISTORY

Let us explore what we now know and do not know. We now know that a Clan Macleay Pipe Band existed in 1912; and perhaps earlier. We know that Portland (Scottish) Pipe Band was formed in either 1903 or 1906, depending upon the source. We know that a number of members of Portland Pipe Band also played with the Canadian Legion Pipe Band.

What we do not know is if there were members of both those bands playing with the then Clan Band. If Harry Fenley's recollection is correct, there was a rift between members of the Portland Pipe Band, which he claims was the formation of the Clan Band, an event Harry stated was "…in the early twenties…." The Clan Lodge's notes talked of David Gray, who played with Portland Pipe Band, and Hugh MacKenzie approaching the Lodge in 1926 with their proposal, which sounded like forming a band which already existed.

As stated, we have gaps and conflicts in what information we have gathered; and we have no contemporaries from the early days, or many of their recollections, on which to fill in some gaps. And even some of what we have conflicts with other information. While we have been fortunate with some discoveries, we are still left to speculate, on some level, to clear up some of the apparent conflicting information and/or gaps.

From what we have thus far gathered, the Clan Band existed in 1912, and perhaps earlier. It also appears that David Gray and others split from the Portland (Scottish) Pipe Band; and that David, along with Hugh MacKenzie, approached the Clan Macleay Lodge for support of some nature, including financial. With Pipe Major John Smith of the Clan Band having died in 1913, perhaps that band was struggling; and we do not know who took over the reins. Perhaps they approached David to take over, and Hugh to manage business. What may have transpired in 1926 was a sort of formalization under David's and Hugh's leadership…a more structured and distinct Clan Macleay Pipe Band to replace a more informal prior entity using the Clan Macleay name. This may have been a form of "reinvigoration" or "reorganization," which term was referenced again decades later. Perhaps David and Hugh could be considered, on some level, as the Clan Band's "saviors," rather than founders.

David Gray, who was referred to in at least one newspaper article as the Clan Band's "co-founder," (which we know was not true) was Pipe Major until at least 1941, after which we lose reference to him.

The earlier-referenced "The Pipe Band" article from 1957 stated that the band was "reorganized in 1954." I do, in fact, recall a conversation with a couple elder members of the Clan Macleay Lodge who claimed that they had formed the band on that date, notwithstanding the fact that the band has continued to exist through all the prior decades, including through the 1940s and WWII. Even more bizarrely, one of those individuals gave me a photograph of the band, taken somewhere between 1934 and 1936. In short, these individuals seemed to dismiss the band's prior history. It's possible, given the article's statement regarding the Clan not having a formal band during WWII, that there was a rift between the Clan Band and the Clan Lodge during that period. But the band clearly existed. So what's the deal?

1954 was the date of the first Tartan Ball of the Clan Band as a fundraiser for uniforms and other needs. And that fundraiser continued until 2007, when it ceased due to the band actually losing money on the event in its final years. The point is that 1954 does appear to represent a form of "reinvention" of the band; perhaps as it did in 1926. We know that Chester MacNeill was Pipe Major in 1949…and perhaps later; and that Duncan MacKenzie, son of the aforementioned Hugh, took over as Pipe Major in c.1952. But was this reinvention, reorganization, or part of the band's cycle?

How Bands Cycle Through Their History: Pipe bands tend to cycle in a number of ways. A number even form, then fold, then re-form. This cycling can be due to growth or atrophy, support or lack thereof, the type of band (e.g., competition-focused vs. parade or performance-focused), and sponsorship, amongst other things. But the most common cycle, especially with longer-lived bands, has to do with numbers; and the Clan Band has gone through many ups and downs in that regard. It's not uncommon, for example, to lose a number of pipers, while maintaining many drummers…or vice versa. I remember when our band was a host band at the Portland Highland Games in the early 1980s at which we had eighteen pipers present. And I've recalled events where we could field no more than six pipers and one side drummer…or even just a

Clan Macleay at the Athena Caledonian Games in Athena, Oregon. P/M John Smith is at left, circa 1912.

tenor or bass. In the late 1980s, most of our drum corps left to join a competition band, leaving us with one side drummer for a few years. And, conversely, in recent years, the band has picked up a number of players from other bands.

Perhaps the references in the band's history to "reorganization" and similar changes related as much to cycling. I've no doubts that the band's numbers during WWII were low, yet the band still existed, notwithstanding other reports. It's likely that the band that existed prior to 1926 was a very small group (and the 1912 photo certainly showed that), and that David Gray, Hugh MacKenzie, and perhaps others, bolstered and gained support and a new life as a larger band.

Yes, there still are gaps to fill, such as who—whether David Gray or another—took charge after the death of John Smith in 1913. The salient point is that the Clan Band is indeed one of the oldest continuously existing pipe bands in the U.S., and perhaps in North America.

Part Two:

OVERVIEW OF THE CLAN BAND

WHAT IS THE CLAN BAND?

THE PREAMBLE TO THE band's current By-Laws state: "The purposes for which the Band is organized are the education in and the playing of Scottish Highland bagpipes and drums, the preservation of piping, drumming and other traditions of Scottish heritage, the encouragement, and the teaching and public performance of bagpipe music at engagements and civic events on a not for profit basis."

These days, there are many adjectives to describe pipe bands…also referred to as bands of pipes and drums. We hear terms like "street band," "performance band," "competition band," "military band," and so forth. Many, like the Clan Band, engage in multiple activities, such as parades and competition, even though they have a primary function or definition.

Throughout its history, the Clan Band has been most appropriately described as a "performance band," although it has engaged in competitions, usually to enhance its level of playing, and thus performance. Up until the late 1990s (when parades starting disappearing), the band was best known for its presence in parades and in other performances. Of the parades, from nearly the beginning of the Grand Floral Parade (aka, Rose Parade) in Portland, the Clan Band was an annual presence and delight of the crowds. But it also appeared for decades in so many smaller town parades in Oregon, and even Washington. As those towns had more financial or other difficulties, or other reasons for the smaller town parades to fade, many of those appearances disappeared. Some, like the Sheridan Days Parade, have continued; though, as of this writing, that, too, appears to have ended (Note: Sheridan deserves special mention in that it was the only town that, for many decades, always had three pipe bands participating, one always being the Clan Band. When I joined, the other two bands were the Eugene Highlanders and the Oregon National Guard Pipe Band; later, other bands, such as Kells Irish Pipes and Drums and Sir James McDonald Junior Pipe Band, participated).

The Clan Band has also participated in a number of other events, such as St. Patrick's Day celebrations, corporate events, ship and barge launches (more on that later), weddings and other private events, and even events for government departments and/or officials.

As mentioned earlier, for 53 years (from 1954 to 2007) the Clan Band also hosted its own fundraiser, the Clan Macleay Tartan Ball. This was also a reciprocal event with a tartan ball hosted by another band from Tacoma, Clan Gordon (which still exists, and at which the Clan Band continued as a guest band, just as Clan Gordon was at the Clan Band's event).

The point is that the band's history has involved a wide array of performances. However, as stated, the band has also often competed in various Highland Games, primarily in the Northwest US and Canada; though often in California, even as far away as

Nova Scotia. Still, the band has retained its identity as principally a performance band.

BY-LAWS, MEMBERS, STRUCTURE AND OFFICERS

If there were By-Laws written at the formation of the band, we do not have them. Regardless of origin, and until it gained its own non-profit tax status, the band operated under the non-profit status of the fraternal society. The current By-Laws—whether reflections of original thoughts/structure, or newly formed—appears to have been drafted in the early 1950s. Of course, there have been modifications to the By-Laws since then; perhaps the most important being the admission of female members (which were not included in the earlier by-laws).

The Clan Band was formed initially for adult males. There were, however, females, many related to band members, who were involved with band performances. These included dancers, such as Bonnie Heather Blyth (MacKenzie), whose father was, at one time, Band Manager. We know, as well, that at least one piper (e.g., the daughter of one of the P/Ms) played with the band in the 1950s. But it appears that none, given the By-Laws at the time, were official members…and perhaps would be considered more as honorary or "ancillary" members (regardless, the dancers especially were an important part of performances).

It was not unusual in the earlier decades of the 20th century that adult bands were all males (and female pipers and drummers were certainly scarcer then, though there were some prominent ones). Over time, more females entered the piping and drumming scene; and, eventually, there even developed all female bands (e.g., Vancouver Ladies; Portland Ladies). However, the Clan Band was all-male for most of its history, even though proposals and votes were taken at periodic band meetings to include females.

Then, in 2001, the band members approved a change to the By-Laws to admit female players. Today, the By-Laws state: "Membership in the Band shall be limited to persons over the age of 16 years. All minor applicants shall obtain written consent of their legal guardian, in the form prescribed by and filed with the Secretary-Treasurer. No person shall be denied membership on account of race, sex, religion or ethnicity". [Note: The band has often had players younger than 16; they are just not eligible for membership until that age]. Whoever the player, prospective members are nominated by a band member at the band's annual meeting (held at the end of the "piping season" in the NW, often in September or early October); usually after the proposed person had played with the band for a season or so. At the time of drafting this work, most of the Clan Band's drum corps, and about one-third of the pipe corps, is female.

There are multiple reasons the Clan Band has practiced nominations of members after the proposed player has invested some time; and it's fair to say that it's also one of the practices that have contributed to the longevity of the band. First, it's important to know if the player is going to be committed and engaged by being prepared and showing up at events. Second, it's as important for the player to know that the band is a fit for him or her; just as it is for the band members to be comfortable with the new person. Third, the band has lost many a good and expensive set of uniforms (referred to as a "kit") to someone outfitted prematurely and absconding with said kit.

As stated, the band has an annual general meeting at the end of the season (and sometimes a special meeting at other times to address any pressing issues). At the general meeting, amongst other proposed agenda items, officers are elected. Elected officers are as follows: Band (Business) Manager; Secretary/Treasurer; Band Historian; and Pipe Major (P/M). Non-elected officers include Drum Major (D/M), Pipe Sergeants (P/S), and Drum Sergeant (D/S)—all appointed by the Pipe Major. There is also a volunteer position of Quartermaster, taking care of and issuing uniforms, chanters and other elements at the direction of the P/M or D/S.

A Nominating Committee presents the slate of the nominated officers at the meeting; and other nominations can be made from the floor. Other committees are the Uniform Committee, Development Committee, and Grievance Committee.

The officers' and others' roles are as follows:

Band (Business) Manager: Responsible for obtaining band events; bringing proposals to the band for votes; writing up contracts; coordinating appearances; and running meetings, including the annual meeting.

Secretary/Treasurer: Takes and keeps meeting minutes; maintains records; handles and reports the band's finances; reviews budget with band officers and members; and issues service and rank stripes and other uniform accoutrements.

Pipe Major: The musical director and primary leader. Appoints non-elected officers and others, namely the Drum Major, Drum Sergeant, Pipe Sergeants, and Pipe Corporals; selects the music, including structuring a medley, quick marches set, and other competition sets; runs band practices/rehearsals; leads the band in competitions and other performances.

Drum Major: Appointed by the P/M. Responsible for deportment and look of the band, including proper wearing of uniform; leads the band in parades and other performances (though cues off P/M's tempos, etc.), through vocal, mace and other signals.

Drum Sergeant: Leader of the drum corps and lead side drummer; constructs and introduces drum scores; appoints others, such as Drum Corporals.

Pipe Sergeant: Takes over for the P/M in his or her absence or at the P/M's requests; assists during practices, helping with tuning and other duties.

Band Historian: Keeps records, photos and other items related to band history; presents items at some events, including band meetings and some appearances.

On the following page is the best we have been able to construct of some of the officers through the years, most of whom are from the early 1950s. Because D/Ss and D/Ms are appointed, and not in band minutes, those dates are estimated:

THE BAND'S LOOK AND UNIFORMS

Like most bands, the band's "look" and uniforms have changed throughout the years. We know that the uniform of the original Portland Scottish/Canadian Legion Pipe Band was that of the 92nd Gordons, which included surplus Gordon kilts from the Second Boer War (1899-1902). It's also reported that the early Clan Band had some of the same regimental kit. The 1912 photograph certainly showed a mish-mash of full dress, various tunics, even Argyle jackets, sporrans, and other individual expressions.

MICHAEL C. HUBBARD

Name	From	To
Pipe Majors:		
Tomas Peralta	2017	Present
Michael Hubbard	1998	2017
David Bueermann	1994	1998
Michael Hubbard	1988	1994
Jeff Brewer	1980	1988
Jack Taylor	1977	1980
Chris Traugh	1974	1977
Doug Speers	1972	1974
Ray Snedden	1964	1972
Newton Muir	1960	1964
David Patterson	1957	1960
Duncan MacKenzie	1952	1957
Chester MacNeill	1941?	1952?
David Gray	1926?	1941?
??	1913	1926?
John Smith	1912?	1913
Drum Majors:		
Linda Mae Dennis	2016	Present
Dan Kelley	2013	Present
George Paterson	1979	2016
William McLellarn	1966	1979
William Lawrence	1963	1964
Drum Sergeants:		
Bill Duncan	2017	Present
Pete Woodall	2009	2017
David Webster	2003	2009
Bruce Riggs	2001	2002
Skip Adams	1989	2001
Ron Galloway	1987	1989
Joe Hewitt	1979	1987
John Waddingham	1972	1979
Ralph Altmans	1964	1972
Eddy Johnson	1960	1964

Name	From	To
Business Managers:		
Karen Woodall	2017	Present
John W. Osburn	2008	2017
Scott Henderson	2004	2008
Ogden Kimberley	2002	2004
Greg Dinse	1998	2002
Howard Cooper	1983	1998
John W. Osburn	1980	1983
Pat Sheaffer	1979	1980
Jerry Durgan	1977	1979
Doug Miller	1974	1977
Pat Sheaffer	1970	1974
Newton Muir	1968	1970
Miles Ralston	1966	1968
Chris Traugh	1964	1966
John Douglas	1962	1964
Bob Blyth	1954?	1962
Hugh MacKenzie	1926	?
Secretary/Treasurers:		
William Farr	1971	Present
Howard Cooper	1966	1971
Ernie Lekas	1964	1966
Tom Lekas	1962	1964
Band Historians:		
Skip Adams	1992	Present
Don Stewart	1992	1997
Bill McCulloch	1990	1992
Ogden Kimberley	1989	1990
Michael Hubbard	1988	1989
John Waddingham	1983	1988
Chuck Huntley	1981	1983
Bill McCulloch	1980	1981
Chuck Huntley	1977	1980
John Waddingham	1970	1977
Duncan MacKenzie	1966	1970
George Ritchie	1964	1966
Howard Cooper	1963	1964
Al Nichols	1962	1963

Full Dress with feather bonnets and glengarry caps, Oregon Governor's inauguration 2008. *Front Row*: D/M George Paterson, Brian MacKenzie, Scott Henderson, Victoria Crowe, David Webster. *Second Row*: Kevin Kelley, Ogden Kimberley, Evan Ackerman, John Osburn, Dan Kelley, Peter Woodall. *Third Row*: Mark Cameron, Bill McCulloch, Kate Elias, P/M Michael Hubbard.

However, as the band eventually gained its own uniforms, the most consistent look has been that of a regimental Scottish band, such as the Scots Guards. Like some of the regimental bands, and unlike most pipe bands these days, the Clan Band still sports two different kilt tartans: Royal Stewart for pipers; Hunting Stewart for drummers. This tradition stemmed from the regimental differentiation in function between the two corps.

The band has had for most of its history, and continues to wear, what would be called Full Dress, or Dress Number 1. This is the classic military look that includes a wool tunic (navy blue for pipers/red for drummers), plaids, cross belts and waist belts, horsehair sporran, spats and feather bonnet (with alternate of glengarry and cock feather). The band has also had variations of the military dress, including white tunics, and the "summer" uniform of short sleeved military shirts. Like most bands these days, the Clan Band also has a "civilian" uniform, which has continued through periodic modifications through the years.

Deportment of the band—including uniformity and proper dress, as well as marching precision—has always been an important part of the band's appearance and in performances. As described, the band's Drum Major is a key figure in ensuring the band's look and carriage.

Another look at Full Dress with Glens, Veterans' Day celebration, Tillamook Air Museum, Tillamook, Oregon, 2012. *Visible, Left to Right*: D/M Dan Kelley, D/S Bill Farr, Steve Hughes, Barry Johnson, Dan Dorsett, Lori Robins, Jeff Robins, and, nearest at right, P/M Michael Hubbard.

Civilian Dress, Portland Highland Games, 2018. D/M Dan Kelley and P/M Tomas Peralta leading band out.

Full Dress with Feather Bonnets, Portland Highland Games, 1978.

Summer Military. Tomas Peralta in Grand Floral Parade 2011.

The following is a series of photos depicting other uniforms and looks from the past:

A mixture of Civilian and Military with shirt and tie, balmorals, horsehair sporrans, and spats, 1958.

Dress whites with pith helmets, 1966. Pipers complained of the pith helmets, for they interfered with the bass drone. They are also quite warm! *Front Row*: D/M William McLellarn, Ralph Altmanns, unk., Miles Ralston, unk., John Waddingham, unk., Joe Hewitt. *2nd Row*: P/M Ray Sneddon, Tom Morton, Jeff Brewer, Doug Miller, unk., Newton Muir, Tom Lekas, Duncan MacKenzie, Howard Cooper, Bruce Phillip. *Back Row*: Colin MacKenzie, unk., unk., unk., Tim Karr, James Wallace.

Civilian with Prince Charlie Coats and glens with cock feathers. Clan Macleay Tartan Ball, 1990.

Khaki shirts and tan balmorals. A short-lived combination in the 1990s. Sheridan Days Parade.

Full Dress with white tunics. Shamrock Run, Portland, OR, 2006.

Band in earlier version of Summer Military, Grand Floral Parade, Portland, OR, 2000. *L to R*: Michael Riedel, Bill Farr, P/M Michael Hubbard, David Brown, Jeff Robins, Mark Cameron, John W. Osburn, Ogden Kimberley, Bill McCulloch, Craig Maxwell, Evan Ackerman, D/M George Paterson.

COMPETITION

As stated earlier, the Clan Band has generally known who and what it is as a performance band. However, for most of its history, the band has still entered competitions, primarily in the Northwest US and British Columbia, Canada. Included in those, of course, has been the Portland Highland Games, where the band has been one of the "home" bands, as had the former Portland Scottish; and, more recently, as have other local, more competition-oriented bands, such as Portland Metro & Metro Junior and Sir James McDonald.

More than meeting crowd expectations for its presence at the Portland Highland Games—where the band has also been the host on multiple occasions—the philosophy of the band toward competition has been utilizing it as an ancillary tool to focus and sharpen skills. In other words, the band has sought objective reviews on the field, from judges and other professionals, to improve overall playing, and thus its other performances.

That said, competition became more of a focus when the talented Jeff Brewer took over as Pipe Major in 1980 (he served in that role until 1988 before co-founding a junior band and also moving on to play in a Grade 1 competition band). Through the 1980s, and until 1994, the band competed in Grade 3 competitions from Canada to Santa Rosa, California (the Caledonia Highland Games, now in Pleasanton). The band even competed a couple times in Nova Scotia (more on that in another chapter). In any event, in the 1980s, the band did exceedingly well in Grade 3 competition; and in 1985, took top prizes in most of its outings in the Northwest.

At the same time, music and band skills in pipe bands were rising dramatically in the 1980s and 1990s, with a lot of focus on competition. Internationally, Canadian, Irish, U.S. and other bands were challenging the traditional and stalwart Scottish competition bands. On regional levels in North America, junior and other competition-oriented bands were coming on the scene more and more, and were influenced by the excellent Grade 1 bands in their areas (e.g., 78th Fraser, Simon Fraser University, Triumph Street, LA Scots, etc.).

As the competition scene changed, coupled with more stringent requirements set by the various associations (e.g., British Columbia Pipe Band Association or BCPA), coordinating more with the Royal Scottish Pipe Band Association (RSPBA), so has the Clan Band's participation. While still viewing competition for its purposes of sharpening skills, the band has been up and down in participation and in grades, going between 3 and 5. However, interest in competition is rising again; and if history proves to repeat, the Clan Band will be on the competition scene more in the future, although still respecting and keeping its identity.

Top: Massed Bands at Portland Highland Games, 2011.
Bottom: Massed Bands, Portland Highland Games, 1979.

SUPPORT AND PROMOTION OF SCOTTISH/CELTIC CULTURE AND OTHER ENTITIES

Somewhat related to the topic of competition, and notwithstanding the Clan Band's primary purpose and personality, there have been some notable developments involving the band and its members…sort of "offspring" in one case; or sponsorship, in others. Regardless, this has been consistent with the band's by-laws of "…the education in and the playing of Scottish Highland bagpipes and drums, the preservation of piping, drumming and other traditions of Scottish heritage, the encouragement, and the teaching and public performance of bagpipe music…"

Mentioned earlier was the band's Tartan Ball, which served as both a fundraiser and an event for the Scottish community in Oregon and SW Washington. The following is a brief history with some information supplied by Colin and Bonnie MacKenzie:

> The Tartan Ball was launched in 1954, principally by Pipe Major Duncan MacKenzie and Tom Jeffries, as a vehicle to raise money for a band which was rebuilding after WWII. Initially, the event was a dinner with the Clan Band and some dancers as entertainment—not unlike many Burns' Night dinners. The original Tartan Ball was at the Eagles Club. [**Note**: As seen in an earlier section, an article in *The Oregonian* stated it was to be held at the Masonic Temple]. *Within a few years, it was under the guidance of Robert Blyth, then band manager of the Clan Band. He moved it to the Palais Royale (on the site of today's Burnside Fred Meyer), where it took on more of today's style as a ball. Generally, this event had been a dress up affair,*

mixing socializing, with ballroom dancing, interrupted periodically with the sounds of pipes and drums and dancing ghillies.

As a fundraiser, the early years often involved raffles and other prizes, including TVs and radios. One year, the Clan Band raffled off a 1956 Dodge donated by one of the local dealers. In addition to these activities, Robert Blyth (father of Bonnie Blyth MacKenzie) began bringing in guest bands. Over the years, The Tartan Ball featured friends from Clan Gordon, a band based in Tacoma, Washington; but also such bands as the Seaforth Highlanders, the Scots Guards and the Irish Rangers.

Returning to the topic of competition, in the 1960s and 1970s, the band had some younger, talented pipers and drummers, including the aforementioned Jeff Brewer, Colin MacKenzie, Joe Hewitt, and others who bolstered a more focused competition direction, and competition corps, within the band. In 1972, those members, along with members of the former Portland Grays Boy's Pipe Band (thought to have been named after David Gray) , led by Jack McGilvary, broke from the Clan Band and formed Oregon's only Grade 1 band to date, Blue Heron Bay Pipe Band. Blue Heron competed successfully, amassing some credible awards from California, including a 1st in Santa Rosa (now the games in Pleasanton) up through British Columbia, before dissolving in 1977—a short life not uncommon with a number of competition bands.

Some years later, in the late 1980s, although through different avenues, another competition band came on the scene. An early start, initially called Pearl Street Pipe Band, added some additional members and became Willamette Valley Pipe Band (not to be confused with today's Willamette

Valley Pipes and Drums, the renaming of another pipe band). It competed in Grade 3, doing quite well in competitions from British Columbia to California, eventually being promoted to Grade 2 by the BCPA before disbanding sometime around 1997. The Clan Band's relationship with Willamette Valley was that it provided some early financial and other support, and even most of its drum corps, as well as a couple pipers (not that the Clan Band was intending to lose members!).

In the early 1980s, members of the Clan Band—including Jeff Brewer, Joe Hewitt, and Michael Hubbard—discussed with others the idea of forming a junior pipe band, although it took years for "critical mass" to develop (that is, enough young players with various instructors who would assist). Eventually, in coordination with other instructors, and with the guidance of Jeff and Robbi Brewer, Joe Hewitt, and Robert McKendrick, a junior band, originally named Oregon Pipers' Society Pipe Band, was formed in 1993. Again, the Clan Band provided some financial and other support, as well as a couple members as instructors. The junior band, eventually renamed Sir James McDonald Pipe Band (in honor of the British Consul to Oregon), became a successful Grade 4 competition band. It even competed in Scotland, winning a number of games (e.g., North Berwick, Perth); and, in 2003 placed 3rd at the World Championships in Glasgow in the Juvenile Grade 4 category.

As it has done historically—whether providing members, instructors, financial aid, or other—the Clan Band has been an active proponent and supporter of other bands and activities promoting Scottish music and culture. This includes band members giving free lessons to those wanting to learn bagpipes or drums, for an instruction program has always been considered essential for the band's future. Many members, past and present, learned from the band.

PERFORMANCES

The Clan Band, at least in the last fifty years or more, has been known primarily for participating in the following, not all of which still exist or in which the band participates these days:

Grand Floral Parade (aka, Portland Rose Parade). As far as is known, the Clan Band participated in this parade from at least near the band's beginning until 2015. In the last several years of its participation, to fill out numbers, the Clan Band asked other bands to join as "friends of Clan Macleay" in the parade. Portland Police Highland Guard was the first band to join the Clan Band in the parade, followed by the formerly named Oregon State Defense Force Band.

Sheridan Days Parade. For as long as our members can remember, Sheridan has not only invited the Clan Band; but has been the only smaller town parade to have multiple pipe bands…traditionally three. And that parade is one of the only ones in which the Clan Band still participated until 2018. Sheridan Days did not occur in 2019, though the hope is that the event, and parade, will commence again.

Various Small Town Parades. There have been so many smaller town parades in the band's history; some of which may still exist, even if the band is no longer a part. Many surrounded events, such as 4th of July, Veteran's Day, or even town celebrations (e.g., anniversary of founding). These have included St. Helens, St. Johns, Cascade Locks, Milwaukie, Gladstone, Hills-

Grand Floral Parade, 2012. Combined Clan Band and then-named Oregon State Defense Force Pipe Band.

Sheridan Days Parade, 1960.

boro, Astoria and Garibaldi, amongst many others. Astoria and Garibaldi deserve more description...

Astoria Regatta and Parade. The band has, on and off, played at this old time and marvelous event, participating in the parade, then usually playing at one or more of several brewpubs, afterwards.

Garibaldi Days Parade. This small coastal town had an equally small parade. Afterward, however, the band would play at pubs from north to south, including The Marina, The Main Deck, the Ghost Hole, and Bozzio's, where it finished up after nearly dragging the whole town and visitors with it.

First place award plaque from the First Annual Oregon Fish Festival, Astoria, Oregon, 1956.

Gunderson Marine Barge Launches. As will be described more in detail later, for the past twenty-five years, the Clan Band has been "Gunderson's Band" to play at, and dedicate, barges built and launched by Gunderson Marine, of Portland.

The band has also played for other events, including ones for Gunderson's parent company, Greenbrier.

St. Patrick's Day Events. Notwithstanding the presumably Scottish roots of the Clan Band, it has always performed at various St. Patrick's Day and surrounding events, including an event called The Shamrock Run (though it eventually turned that event over to another pipe band). For decades, the band was split between Jake's Crawfish and McCormick & Schmick's in downtown Portland. After the downtown McCormick's closed, the band has continued at Jake's, as well as at other sites, including J.B. O'Brien's pub.

Robert Burns Dinners. For many years, the Clan Band was the featured performer at the Clan Macleay Lodge's Burns dinners. For many years, they were held at the Masonic Temple on S.W. Park in Portland (which is now part of the Portland Art Museum). It was quite the event through the 1980s, but became smaller, moving to one of the Elks Club venues until the event disappeared. Related to the Lodge, one or two members of the band would also play at installation of new Clan Macleay Lodge members.

Highland Weekend. For a number of years in the summer, Timberline Lodge hosted a "Highland Weekend," featuring the band, dancers and other Scottish-themed performances, mostly done outside. Timberline was also the location for a few Portland Highland Games.

A Highland Evening in the Park. Again, for a number of years in the 1980s, the band was one of the featured performers, along with Highland dancers, fiddlers and others, in the outdoor arena near the Portland Rose Gardens. It was one of the

Taking a break at Jake's Crawfish, St. Patrick's Day. *L to R*: Alex Smith, George Paterson, Steve Hughes and Dan Dorsett.

programs hosted by Parks and Recreation. The band usually performed twice; first in one uniform, like summer military or civilian, then would go behind a large hedge and change into Full Dress to return for the finale.

Memorial Day and Veterans' Day Parades/Events. The Clan Band has participated in many different events surrounding these two holidays of recognition. The most common were events at two different cemeteries/memorials...one in the Sellwood part of Portland, and one in Hillsboro. More recently, the band has been invited by the former Oregon Defense Force band, now called Willamette Valley Pipes and

CLAN BAND

Highland Weekend at Timberline Lodge, mid-1960s.

Veterans' Day at Tillamook Air Museum, Tillamook, Oregon, 2012.

Drums, to join them in the very large Veterans' Day Parade in Albany, Oregon.

Oregon Pipers Society (OPS). Since OPS's formation in 1987, the Clan Band, like other bands, has agreed to perform as a guest band, on occasion. The society meets every third Saturday, from October through April, and often features solo competitions, local performers, invited professional performers, and pipe bands and other groups.

Clan Band performance at OPS, February 2019.

TUNES, PRACTICES, AND REHEARSALS

Like many bands, the Clan Band's tune list has generally consisted of traditional Scottish, Irish and other Celtic tunes, although it has also incorporated newer compositions, including some that band members have scored. The band has always had an annual tune list, modified each season. It has generally included the season's tunes, tunes that all should know (e.g., so-called "massed bands" tunes, like "Scotland the Brave"), a medley, a quick marches set (QMS), and perhaps an MSR (march, strathspey and reel). The list is usually put together by the P/M, ideally with input from the D/S, given that drummers need to come up with scores for the selected tunes (many years ago, drummers often played "massed bands" scores for the tunes; but the band now requires drum scores for each tune).

Most Clan Band P/Ms have kept the list reasonable in size (e.g., twenty tunes), recognizing quality over quantity…as well as what can be reasonably given time in practices. Experience has shown that for a band of its level and nature, a tune list beyond, say, twenty to twenty-five tunes does not benefit; and, in fact, can be counter-productive. Of course, most pipers know many more tunes beyond just the band's selections. Yet another reason for a limited list is that the band has, as stated earlier, drum scores for each tune. In any event, the list generally consists of marches of various time signatures (e.g., 2/4, 3/4, 4/4, 6/8), "dance" tunes (e.g., Strathspey, reel, hornpipe), and slow aires/hymns (e.g., "Amazing Grace"), as well as sets (e.g., marches selection) and medleys of mixed marches and dance tunes.

Like most bands, practices may involve practice chanters and drum pads—especially while learning tunes—being "on the floor" with pipes and drums, or a combination of both types of practices. Marching while playing is also a necessity for parades and other performances; and also includes musical routines, such as those for the various tartan balls.

Regarding practice sessions and locations, the band has usually practiced one night per week. When competition or some performances are approaching, the band has occasionally gone to two rehearsals per week. As for locations, pipe bands

Pipe Major Tomas Peralta leading practice session at Calvary Presbyterian Church in Tigard, Oregon, 2019.

tend to find it difficult to have a permanent home. Whether that's due to noise, logistics, or other factors, the Clan Band has had multiple "homes," especially during the fall through spring. In the summer, practices have often been outside; sometimes at a school or church parking lot or at a park.

For indoor practices, in the 1950s the band actually had practices in a pub, at a member's home, and even on a member's houseboat. Since the 1960s, the band has had practice locations at a minimum of five schools and one church. Schools, with gymnasiums and other areas with enough room for marching practices, have been the best spots. However, the periods with the schools usually end up being finite. Sometimes, that's been due to the school no longer wanting the noise; but mostly due to schools, through Parks & Recreation, starting to charge fees for use that are beyond the band's budget. As with any pipe band, orchestra, or other musical group, the band has always been grateful for any home.

INSTRUMENTS

As with many bands, and as somewhat covered in an earlier section, there is substantial history with a number of instruments—primarily the bagpipes—played in the Clan Band. Bagpipes have always been supplied by, and obviously the property of, the individual piper. Drums, which include sides, tenors and bass, have generally been supplied by the band, as are replacement heads, harnesses, and other parts.

As for the drums, there has been an evolution over the years. Side, tenor and bass drums were originally wood framed, rope tensioned, with hide skin heads. Today's drums are usually constructed of wood and/or synthetic materials, tensioned with bolts, nuts and other metal hardware, and with mostly various types of synthetic heads. Over the years, the Clan Band has purchased and played drums from a variety of drum manufacturers.

Bagpipes are in an entirely different category. As stated, they are owned by the piper; and in the Clan Band, they run the gamut of makers…and histories. Most are from bagpipe makers in Scotland, though some are from Ireland, Canada, and the U.S. (including a well-known maker in Oregon), with names, such as Center, Lawrie, Henderson, Robertson, Hardie, Kintail,

Kilgour, McCallum, Sinclair, Colin Kyo and many others, represented in the band. In the Clan Band, some are fairly new, many are vintage, and a few have been passed down through the families. Of the vintage and/or heritage pipes, they have been as old as late 19th century (e.g., Center); some from the 1920s and '30s; and quite a few from the 1950s and '60s. The band has also received kindly donated bagpipes—some from former members—that the band has been able to loan to students or sell to some other worthy piper.

Most bagpipes in the early 20th century forward have been made from African Blackwood, although some from Ebony and other dense woods (See earlier History section). The value lay more with the maker, history, and especially with ornamentation. Ornamenting can be with various metals (nickel, silver, brass), with various imitation ivories (e.g., early versions, like Catalin, and more recent, and better, plastics), some with ivory, including pre-convention elephant ivory, mastodon ivory, some with bone or other materials, and some with wood (with more modern versions using some interesting woods, such as Purple Heart).

Those with elephant ivory have been of more recent concern due to CITES (the Convention on International Trade in Endangered Species of Wild Fauna and Flora). Elephant ivory used on pipes that are allegedly exempt from restriction or confiscation are pre-convention, meaning prior to the 1970s CITES against the trade of products from endangered species (mastodon ivory, given it comes from an extinct animal, is exempt). Consequently, players in the US and Canada, as well as some other countries, with pipes ornamented with ivory usually apply for a CITES permit, proving the ivory is pre-convention.

However, even with such permits, pipers have become increasingly hesitant to cross international boundaries, such as attending games in other countries (e.g., U.S. pipers traveling to Canada or the UK or vice versa). This stems from "horror stories" of family and other vintage pipes being confiscated by border authorities, never to be seen again (or at least the owner going through a nightmarish process of reclaiming). This has not been limited to bagpipes, for other musicians have had similar issues. For example, some violin, viola and cello bows have ivory tips and other parts on them, as have other orchestra instruments.

Returning to the topic of band bagpipes, each Clan Band member is responsible for other parts, including pipe bags, which include sheepskin, cowhide, and some synthetic hybrids or others. They also purchase their own drone reeds. While some bands have played with matching drone reeds (i.e., all the same make), our experience has been that there is no "one fits all"; so each member selects what works for their particular drones. Drone reeds, like chanter reeds, used to be cane. However, while some still use cane, many pipers have switched to the many different "synthetic" drone reeds.

The band, however, provides matched bagpipe chanters and chanter reeds (still cane, even though there are now some synthetic ones available). The matching of chanters and reeds makes for much easier and consistent tuning, as well as consistency of tone.

In short, the band's history is matched with those of the instruments played through the many years. The sad thing is the realization that there are many wonderful vintage bagpipes, whether from former members or others, that could be played, yet sit under beds, in closets, or—perish the thought—nailed over fireplace mantles.

GUNDERSON/GREENBRIER

The Clan Band's more recent history could not be at all complete without discussion of its relationship with Gunderson Marine, and its owner, Greenbrier Corporation. In the mid-1990s, Greenbrier's Chairman and CEO, Bill Furman, with Celtic heritage, had a vision of having a bagpipe band play at certain events, including the launching of barges made by Gunderson Marine.

Launch of "Prometheus" with D/M George Paterson in front. Photo by Harold Hutchinson.

Gunderson Marine barge launch in 2010 in brisk winds and rain. Band is playing *Amazing Grace* and Drum Major George Paterson out front. Photo by Harold Hutchinson.

The initial barge launch, where the band played at the gate, then led the crowd down to the barge, was met with very curious looks from employees and guests. Gunderson's employees have been rather ethnically diverse, and from the reaction to our playing, many clearly had never heard a bagpipe, let alone an entire pipe band.

Curious though it may have started, the employees and guests became more familiar with the band and ceremony; the relationship with Gunderson/Greenbrier bonded, and has become one of the most important and treasured in the band's history. It has constituted the closest to a sponsorship, without being one formally, with significant financial importance to the band. Yet it is also viewed as one of mutual friendship and devotion, and it's led to some wonderful events and stories (some covered later). That said, at Gunderson/Greenbrier events, the band is generally introduced as "Gunderson's (or Greenbrier's) Own." The band even plays a tune a composed by P/M Michael Hubbard, named "Clan Macleay Salute to Gunderson/Greenbrier."

Another launch, looking up at barge and riders. Seen in photo: Karen Woodall on tenor, Kevin Kelley on bass, and piper Mark Cameron. Photo by Harold Hutchinson.

CLAN BAND

Part Three:
CLANECDOTES*
Stories and Anecdotes

INTRODUCTION

THE BAND, GIVEN ITS history, is understandably rich with stories and anecdotes. Some are very funny, some embarrassing, and some sad; but all reflect the history and nature of the Clan Band. Invariably, whenever the band gathers, whether in pubs after parades or in other venues, anecdotes emerge. New members, especially, are generally regaled by tales, whether embellished or not; and some stories are now lost. So it's only right to have a portion of this work that consists of some tales that we can recall. Consequently, this section is a collection of contributions from various members—former or current—relatives and friends of the band, tales handed down, and so forth. They are not chronological or organized in any other way; so they cover various time periods and events. Those not labeled with a "Submitted by…" are the author's recollections.

---

* Thanks to Linda Mae Dennis for the clever "Clanecdotes" name.

FIRST GIGS

Even though I grew up going to Highland Games with family (Upstate New York), and always wanted to learn the pipes, I didn't start lessons until I was 30 years old and after moving to Oregon. I was introduced to Pipe Sergeant Howard Cooper by a mutual friend and former member of the band, Tom Lekas.

Howard was an excellent instructor, and I was on pipes fairly quickly, then nervously sitting in practice sessions with the band soon after. Like so many learning, I was anxious to be outfitted and to play with the band. But, just like any other wannabe, I had to earn my place in the ranks; which meant I had to know all the tunes and play them to the P/M's satisfaction.

I did get my chance, but not as a piper—a position I had not yet earned. Rather, it was as a drummer (well, sort of). Around 1980/81, the band had put together a four man sword dance as one of its performances. I took dance lessons with other members with the Bonnie MacKenzie Dance Company; and, to get me on the floor, the band strapped a tenor drum on me and taught me some rudimentary flourishes. As an aside, today we consider tenor drums as contributing band instruments more than we did back then. However, it was a way to get me on the floor while I was learning the pipe tunes and working to be a piper in the band.

I don't recall the setting, though I believe it was at Willamette University in Salem, Oregon. In any event, we were putting on a performance in a gymnasium, marching back and forth, and it was my first time out. I had been working on looking good in a drummer's uniform and doing decent flourishes (the drum—an old rope tension one—had the sound of wet cardboard; so I was not to play!). But I was not well-schooled, yet, in marching and I was very nervous.

As we marched onto the floor, I sidled up next to the bass drummer, Lynn Easton, perhaps for comfort. Lynn, a talented musician, was drumming away, yet saying something to me that I couldn't quite understand. Finally, he yelled out, "Get away from me. Move over!" I realized that I was so close that I was nearly hugging him, interfering with his left arm and drumming.

In the following spring, after I'd learned the pipe tunes, my instructor suggested to P/M Jeff Brewer that I was ready for an upcoming parade. Jeff was dubious; but at the time, the band had a policy of requiring at least nine pipers before committing to a parade. The St. John's parade was coming up, and we only had eight pipers committing. My instructor recommended me to fill out the requirement, and Jeff agreed to put me in. So I was outfitted now as a piper.

Like many others, I'm sure, I was so excited and proud to dress up, have photos taken by my wife, and ready to show up at the event in full dress, certain that I looked just right. When I arrived at the event, the band members started laughing. No, I didn't have my kilt on backward (I at least knew how a kilt was worn), something we'd seen so many others do. More minor, yet still humorous, is that I had my spats on with the buttons on the inside…in other words, backwards.

Another piper, John W. Osburn ("John W," for his son, another piper, is "John R."), was kind enough to pull them off and re-button them properly (back then, before Velcro, spats were buttoned up tediously). Anyway, all set to go, I was positioned in the back rank, next to another Pipe Sergeant, Jimmy Wallace (who later left to become P/M of the then Oregon National Guard Pipe Band). Jimmy was very encouraging, talking me through the marching. I needed that, for I was so focused on remembering and playing the tunes, that all else was numb.

I got through my first parade as a piper with everyone's help. But that's also when I realized that the bagpipe is an instrument of increasing distraction. One may think he or she knows a tune; but combine piping, marching, and having a crowd around, it certainly shakes up one's confidence, sometimes manifested in forgetting how the tune goes!

Post-script: I learned a while ago that those of us who've played a long time benefit by tapping vicariously into the emotions and excitement of newer players. Their wide-eyed perspective can be energizing, reminding us of our first times and the wonderment of the experience.

MY CLAN MACLEAY MEMORY: *SUBMITTED BY KATIE NORDONE (BASS DRUMMER)*

Every June since about 1964 my Mom took my brother and me to watch the Rose Parade (now called the Grand Floral Parade). She'd tote snacks, activities and books to keep us occupied while we waited for the parade to start. We'd sit on the curb for hours! In my memory it was often rainy or foggy.

Every year you could hear the pipe band coming from blocks away. Bagpipes are especially effective in the gloom. The excitement would build—the Clan is coming! Soon the white spats could be seen. The pipers led the band in their full dress.

The red tartans and feather bonnets were impressive! The drum section seemed huge as it thundered behind the pipes. Truly awesome! That was the highlight of the parade for me each year.

When I was asked to sub in the band a few years ago the first person I called was my Mom. When I told her I was going to play with the Clan Macleay she was ready to get her ticket to the parade!

I am honored to be a member of this band.

ROSE PARADE ARTICLE WRITTEN (AND ART) BY JOHN WADDINGHAM: *SUBMITTED BY DAVID DAY*

Un-merry Merrykhana
Parade, hah! It was only a water fight

By JOHN WADDINGHAM
Art Director, The Oregonian

Editor's Note: The writer is a Clan Macleay drummer who marched, skidded and got soaked in the Merrykhana Parade.

THE ANNUAL Merrykhana Parade held last Saturday evening was the wettest in history.

In speaking of wetness, we don't mean the usual Oregon mist that seems to plague Rose Festival parades. We mean water-balloon wetness.

The spirit of good, clean fun has always been a part of the Merrykhana Parade and no members of the Clan Macleay Pipes and Drums minded getting a squirt or two of water from mischievous curbside spectators. This has always been a part of it. Clan members play their pipes and drums as though oblivious to the squirts from water guns, usually aimed at bare knees under the kilts. Who can blame the kids? Maybe we'd do the same thing if the tables were reversed.

Still, put yourself in the place of some of the parade marchers and float participants last Saturday night.

Not content with a few water balloons filled with clean water, the curbside rowdies ran out in front of the families that had held down a viewing spot for hours and doused marchers and float riders with containers of filthy water scooped up out of the gutters. Such gutters were awash from fire hoses squirted back in defiance by volunteer fire groups and other parade participants.

In some cases, teen-age boys

dumped half gallon milk cartons full of filthy water over the uniforms, ostrich feather headgear, and, incidentally, the faces of Clan Macleay pipers and drummers, who marched on, gritting their teeth and smiling.

After all, it was only the renegades and not the generally appreciative crowd who were doing the damage. Yet it turned a fine parade into nothing more than a pro-longed "bath."

Many other parade participants had spent hours preparing colorful costumes, only to have them ruined by filth. Every parade block there seemed to be a gang of young rowdies soaking newspapers and paper towels in the gutter, ready to fling them on some lovely young girls on a float or into a marching group.

After awhile, it wasn't a parade anymore. Just a water fight between the spectators and parade participants with the hoses.

If the Clan Macleay participates next year, I think we will have added a battle decoration emblazoned on our drums.

It will read: "Merrykhana, 1972."

And we may be wearing raincoats over our kilts.

SOLEMNITY INTERRUPTED

This occurred sometime around 1985, give or take a year, at the Caledonian (Club of San Francisco) Highland Games, then in Santa Rosa, California (they now take place in Pleasanton). Our band was there to compete. Following competition was the massed bands—at the time, some forty-five to fifty of them—in which the bands would march onto the race track between the grandstand and the inner field and come to attention. This would normally be the moment when the band competition results would be announced for each grade, and then the gathered bands would play a tune or two, often including "Amazing Grace."

With all the bands now gathered on the track, and the crowd in the bandstand watching in awe over hundreds of pipers and drummers, the announcer, who was at a table set up in the inner field on the other side of the wood railings, announced that the Scots Guards were present.

His reverberating voice, echoing off the grandstands, said that before results were to be announced, the massed bands would play "Amazing Grace" in honor of all who were no longer with us. Further, he announced that the Pipe Major of the Scots Guards would lead off with a solo, to be joined by the massed bands. Silence came over the field for this solemn event.

Seconds before the solo piper started, there was a sudden loud KAWAAM!, interrupting all and echoing throughout the stadium. Everyone, from massed band participants to the spectators, snapped their heads to the inner field. There was a "port-a-potty" unfortunately situated right behind the announcer's table; and a man, holding a beer can, had emerged at that solemn moment and let the spring-hinged door slam. He appeared to be oblivious to the ongoing event, for he staggered over to the railing, set his beer can on it, and leaned on the fence to watch.

Laughter broke out amongst the massed bands and spectators, and any serious moment was broken. I imagine that if this gentleman had any relatives in the stands, they likely died of shame.

THE PINNING: *SUBMITTED BY BRAD COLLINS*

While on official Educational Leave from the Clan Gordon Pipe Band so I could attend graduate school at OSU (Oregon State University), I joined the Clan Macleay Pipe Band from 2006 to 2009. I enjoyed playing with the Clan Band very much and made a lot of friends there.

Practices and performances were usually fun and well worth the trip up from Corvallis, but the experience wasn't without blood, sweat, and tears. One evening, while prepping for the Annual Clan Gordon Tartan Ball, we were downstairs in the pavilion getting the final pieces of our uniform in shape. I asked Geordie Paterson [our D/M at the time] to wrap my plaid and secure my brooch, and he obliged as he always did.

He wrapped the folds of the plaid expertly and then grabbed the brooch. In retrospect, I'm glad I had a little anesthesia in my blood stream because he jabbed the pin of the brooch through the plaid, through my tunic, through my t-shirt, and through most of the muscle of my shoulder. I swear it came out the other side, but I didn't see an exit wound. I howled, hissed, and swore several oaths, but Geordie was unfazed. After finally getting the pin secured the correct way, he said something like, "Och, just put pressure on it," and walked away. I still have the t-shirt with a small hole and a large blood stain. Good times.

NOVA SCOTIA ADVENTURE

As described earlier, Greenbrier, which owns Gunderson Rail and Marine, sort of adopted the band as its own for their events. Sometime in the 1990s, Greenbrier purchased Trenton Works, a railcar building business, located in New Glasgow, Nova Scotia. Greenbrier's Chairman and CEO, Bill Furman, wanted to celebrate the purchase by sending the Clan Band to play at Trenton Works. When I told Bill that there were dozens of bands in NS, he said, "Yes, but you're *our* band, and I want you to represent us."

Greenbrier was exceedingly generous, flying us there and taking care of everything. When we landed and drove to New Glasgow, we discovered a marvelous old pub, named The Dock. At the time, many of us were enjoying a certain kind of beer (as I recall, it was Caffrey's Irish Cream Ale), and we drank the pub out of it. I remember the owner saying, "Why didn't you guys tell us you were coming? I'd have had more on hand." The next day, the owner drove to Halifax to buy up all of it he could find—though all that was available was in cans—just in case we returned (which we did).

The next day, we played at Trenton Works to an otherwise confused group of employees; and we were due to play, later that evening, at some other venue. However, we discovered that there was a Highland games and band competition in Antigonish, and that we could enter on the field. So we hopped in our cars and caravanned it up to Antigonish, entering their Grade 3 competition. It was simply a four-part march, and we took 2nd place.

We had to high-tail it back to New Glasgow to perform at another event; so we took our check, hopped in the cars and got back just in time to play. We ended up also playing with another band, the Heatherbelle Girls Pipe Band. Afterward, we went back to The Dock where the owner allowed us to sign over our check from the competition toward beer and food. I think the check was for around CAD$250. As we were getting ready to leave, we were presented with a bill in excess of $300…and that was after subtracting the $250!

Post-script: There was a humorous and unexpected event at the competition in Antigonish. When we marched onto the field, we saw that one of the judges was Bob Worrall. Just weeks before, Bob had been in Oregon to put on a workshop at the Oregon Pipers' Society. Because we'd entered on the field, we were not on the program; and when we were announced, Bob did the best double-take we'd ever seen. After all, what were the odds of a band from Oregon showing up at a small competition in Nova Scotia? In fact, we were introduced as being from Portland, Maine! But Bob knew who we were, and his look was priceless.

MY CLANECDOTES: *SUBMITTED BY JEFF ROBINS*

Clanecdote 1: The year—2001. It was my first time participating in the Clan Gordon Tartan Ball. We had performed already and were enjoying the event over scotches, beers or whatever beverage we had decided was the choice for the evening.

While doing so, the dance band played on and we simply were enjoying the camaraderie that is so appreciated with this band. Then it was time for the Tacoma Scots band to play and as is customary, some of us moved toward the floor to have a better listen.

It was very warm in the room and the "Scots" seemed to be playing a very long set. Suddenly, there was "a piper doon." One of the Tacoma band members had collapsed in the circle. People rushed over to attend to her. I was standing with Bill Farr, MD, and I happen to be a technologist in an interventional cardiovascular lab. With a scotch in my hand and if I recall correctly, a beer in Bill's hand, Farr looks at me and says (loosely quoted), "I guess the professional thing to do would be to see if she is okay."

So we began walking toward the person in distress to find a somewhat panicking individual yelling at others to back up as she was an RN. Witnessing that exchange was enough for Farr to look at me and say, "She's good," before turning and walking away.

Clanecdote 2: Saint Patrick's Day at the old McCormicks and Schmicks location in downtown Portland. Julie, a prospective member, had come to listen. Mind you, Julie is all of 5 feet tall. We had marched in and were in the bar area where Julie was seated at the counter. A gentleman next to her noticed former member and I believe, the first female piper and mentioned his surprise that there was a woman in the band. Julie was immediately in the guy's face, pointing her finger at him and showing that with a few drinks and the right button pushed, she could become quite "animated." I mentioned to P/M Michael Hubbard that it seemed the band had gained a little wiener dog.

Fast forward to the Sheridan Parade later that year. Julie had successfully learned the tunes and was invited to march in the parade with us as her first event with the band. We learned that day that even without a few drinks or without any buttons being pushed, she could also be animated. As she was stressing over the parade, she was pacing back and forth unable to be calmed down. Michael finally looked at me and said, "Do you think she's allowed on the furniture at home?"

Clanecdote 3: In 2009 or 2010, the band travelled to Mt Vernon for the Skagit Valley Highland Games. On the drive up, I had gone through a drive through to grab a bite for the road. It was at a Jack in the Box and for reasons unknown to me at the time, I had a strong urge to purchase one of the famous Jack antenna balls—essentially, s styrofoam clown head.

Saturday came and we enjoyed a day of visiting in the band tent, competing as a band, and enjoying cold beer in the beer tent courtesy of the Skagit Valley Brew Pub. It was after a few of their very tasty Scottish ales that the reason my urge to buy the clown head came to me.

We heard the announcement that massed band would soon be assembling, so we left the beer tent and returned to the band tent to retrieve our instruments. I proceeded to retrieve my pipes and also the antenna ball. I then, before D/M George Paterson returned, placed the antenna ball atop of St. Andrew's head which adorned the top of Geordie's mace. Keep in mind that I fully believed he would notice before we left the band tent. Rather, he didn't notice it at all and Michael Hubbard and I didn't see any reason to say anything about it.

So massed bands begins and George marches us in along

with the other bands and other Drum Majors. It should be noted that we were, in fact, due to the proximity of the Canadian border, marching in with bands who regularly competed in the world championships, including the reigning champions, SFU.

All the bands marched in together, and at the halt, Geordie brings his mace down in front of him. It seemed as though his eyes crossed at the moment he saw the clown head. He then tipped the mace to one side, looked down our file and uttered the words I'll never forget: "Who's been feckin' with my mace?" We played well that day but didn't place. However, that incident is one of my proudest moments with the band.

THE BORDER CROSSING

I believe this incident occurred in April 1984; and it involved two of us young pipers returning from a competition, commonly called the "BC Indoor," in Vancouver, British Columbia. This event, held on Easter weekend, is an all-day affair of individual piping and drumming competition in the morning and afternoon, followed by band competitions in the evening.

In any event, Allan Muir (whose father was P/M decades before) and I were traveling and rooming together as part of the competition corps of the Clan Band. On Sunday, the day after the BC Indoor (and I don't recall how the band finished in competition, other than we competed in Grade 3), he and I decided to get up early in the hopes of beating a crowd at the border crossing into Washington State. And we were pleased to arrive with very little traffic waiting to cross.

Now these were not days generally associated with fears of

terrorist attacks. I'm sure the border guards were more concerned with drug possession or trafficking, contraband, or other illegal activities. Still, whether through random selection, or suspicion over two unshaved guys in t-shirts and jeans driving an Audi, we were asked to pull over to a designated spot for inspection. The guard also said, "Leave the keys in the car and enter the building over there."

It's important in this story to know that my friend and bandmate, Allan, was a very good attorney who argued most of his cases in the appellate courts in Oregon. So when we parked and got out of the car, Allan, being the typical attorney, turned to me and asked, "Do you think we have a constitutional right to observe the search?"

As I was responding with, "I don't know," the same guard saw us lingering and came running over, pointing and screaming loudly, "I told you two to get in that building." I said to Allan, "Well, I'm going in. You can argue about the search if you'd like." As I approached the door, I looked back and saw Allan, considerably taller than the guard, leaning over, talking and shaking his finger for emphasis. I went in and sat down.

About ten minutes later, Alan walked in, looking a bit deflated, and sat down next to me. I said, "What happened?" Allan, in a low voice, said, "They didn't want to hear about The Constitution."

Neither Allan nor I were into drugs or anything illicit (although I am glad that I put the empty beer cans from the car floor into the trash back at the motel!). Nor were we trying to get anything across the border, except for our tired bodies. Then again, our lingering, along with Alan's insistence, likely heightened some suspicion in the guards. But, upon their search, the guards clearly saw the law journals on the passenger side; for when the official came in, he referenced some journal article and was pleasant and engaging. That said, the experience was also a lesson that we have very few to no rights in that "zone" of the border crossing.

Post-script: Today, the fear for many pipers in border crossings has more to do with any of us who have ivory decorations on our pipes. No matter if we have CITES permits (proving pre-convention ivory) and/or pipes handed down through generations, there is always a fear of an over-zealous border guard confiscating our most valued instrument.

BUSTED! TOLD BY JOE HEWITT AND BONNIE MACKENZIE

Normally, we've avoided stories that are rather embarrassing. However, Joe shared this, laughing at his recollection. The story relates to how many times we've seen those who don a kilt, sport what they believe a Scottish, Irish, or other accent, and pretend to be something they're not, whether to "attract the girls," as the saying goes, to play a role—perhaps during a Renaissance festival—or just to have some playacting fun.

In any event, as Joe tells it, he was a drumming student in the band; and, like many students, was anxious to be part of the culture and all. The Grand Floral Parade was on; and while Joe couldn't be part of the band, yet, he and a friend decided to look the part. I'm not certain if the friend was also a student, or just a bloke who was talked into the role playing. But they somehow secured kilts, but no other Highland garb.

To look more the part, they donned Boy Scout hose and shirts and made something resembling sporrans. Joe wanted to have something that looked like spats; so they cut up long white socks and pulled them over their shoes. I'm not sure what else they managed to imitate; but off they went to strut around the crowd getting ready for the parade. Joe decided that they would pretend to be part of a Canadian legion; so, with their best imitation of a Canadian accent, eh?, they made themselves conspicuous, walking along the street. Joe admits that he assured his friend that this would attract the girls, too.

At one point, Joe and his friend had a group around them, regaling them with their stories, when Colin and Bonnie MacKenzie, who were watching the parade from a vantage point higher up, noticed them. They decided to go down. Joe recalls that he was in the middle of some tale, when he suddenly saw Bonnie's face, after she'd moved through the crowd. He then heard her say, very loudly, "Hello, Joe!" Busted! But not entirely out of the woods as he and his friend excused themselves and sidled out the other direction.

As Joe explained it, they ran square into an old Scotsman and former Pipe Sergeant of another band. The old gentleman looked at them, then down at their handmade sporran, Boy Scout hose, and stretched white sock "spats." He bellowed out, "What the foock!" They were not only busted, but now totally deflated.

Post-Script: Joe not only became a valuable member and Drum Sergeant of the band. He was also a member of a number of excellent bands, co-founder of a youth band, and was a valued instructor. In addition, Joe became an expert on regimental uniforms, cap badges, and other historical elements. His passing was a blow to so many, and he is sorely missed.

COMPETITION COMEDY: WOES AND REWARDS

I'll start with a woe: My first solo competition. I was playing a 2/4 march, called "Hugh Kennedy." It's a lovely tune; but in reflection, perhaps not the best choice for a novice. In any event, I was playing well and was into the fourth part, which has an alternate ending on the repeat—which had also been a weak spot in my practices.

Just as I approached that alternate ending phrase, I looked up to see a co-worker of mine walking toward me down the track. Poor timing, and a big mistake for me to look around! I had a major choke and was undone (or I guess simply done). The judge's sheet had great comments and compliments… until, in large letters, it said, "Broke down."

In contrast, some pipers just seem to have no nerves. A bandmate, the very same attorney, Allan, in another story, is one who often pulled a rumpled uniform from the trunk of his car (see a later anecdote). At the Portland (Oregon) Highland Games one year, he showed up on the field just as the steward was searching for him. His pipes were still in the case, and he was up. While the steward was rather agitated, Allan just pulled out his pipes, barely tuned them, and walked into the competition area and played his march. He took 1st place.

Speaking of competition "areas," often called "platforms," they vary for solo contests. Some are indeed platforms of wooden decks. Many others are roped-off areas in which there is a table and chair, sometimes with an umbrella, for the judge. Such has usually been the set-up at the Portland Highland Games. And the usual convention is to enter when the judge nods that he or she is ready, introduce yourself, indicate what you will be playing, and wait for the judge to acknowledge that you can start.

At one of the Portland solo piping competitions, another bandmate, Pat, walked into the platform with a can of beer. Instead of following convention, he set the can on the table in front of the startled judge and said, "Will you watch that for me?" He then promptly went into his competition tune. I don't recall how he did; but after the initial shock, the judge appeared more amused than irritated.

Bands are not immune to all sorts of issues; and we've had most of them. Chanters, not tight enough, popping out; bags suddenly losing air (e.g., I recall my instructor's bag "popping" during competition); and reeds going out of tune are just a few examples. I recall our band competing at the Skagit Valley Games one time and coming up to the line. Bands typically play a tune up to the line where a steward is standing to let the band know when it can march into its medley, MSR, or whatever the competition is. We were doing a medley, and I made the mistake of not humming the opening tune (what we call the "attack" tune). We rolled off, and two people behind me started in on the tune we had just played up to the line! That pretty much blew the attack and any chances of placing.

At another games competition, one piper, who seemed to have perennial problems with his pipes, also appeared to have them at the most inopportune times. At one in Portland, the steward came to the tent to let us know it was time to go down on the field to be on deck. This same piper tripped over a tent line and fell on his pipes. Worse, when we were on deck, getting a final check on tuning, his bass drone stock popped out of the bag. Naturally, he was cut (and we were fortunate it happened on deck, and not during competition).

In regard to competition, I prefer competing in a band

setting to solo. But in solo competition, the thrill of a student's success on any level is the most rewarding for me, and beats any other achievement. Of all the rewards I've felt from a student's accomplishment, my favorite experience was in the first win for Olivia, who I think was around eleven years old at the time.

She was just about to turn nine when I took her on as a student, and as part of the instruction program of Sir James McDonald Pipe Band, a junior band in Portland (originally named Oregon Pipers Society Junior Pipe Band). When Olivia was finally on pipes, and competing with all her peers, she was playing well at competitions. But she was not placing; and it was frustrating her.

Toward the end of the season, I talked her mother into bringing Olivia to a very small event in Kelso, Washington, (Kelso Highlander Festival) that had solo piping competition. They did come, and Olivia entered two events, a march and a slow aire. She did beautifully in her march, but her F collapsed (meaning it suddenly played ear-jarringly flat); I felt awful, for it was not her fault. I fixed the reed and she played her slow aire, again doing well (and the reed cooperated).

Her mother took Olivia to get some ice cream, and I waited with others for the announcement of the results (this was a small event, so the placings were just announced, rather than posted). The judge announced Olivia's name for 1st in the slow aire, and I came forward to get her prize and to find her and her mother. I found them approaching, Olivia working on an ice cream cone, and I held up the medal. Her face brightened and she took the medal.

At the next band practice, her mother told me that Olivia

slept with her medal. The following season, she took aggregate (overall winner in a grade) in the Bellingham Games, as well as others. She is a Grade 1 piper today, married and living in Scotland.

Post-script: When my original instructor died, his pipes (1960's Hardie) were given to me, which I turned over to the band to sell. Olivia's family bought them, and she used them very effectively for many years.

FORGOTTEN PARTS

It's not uncommon in any band for some members showing up at a gig sans some part of their uniform. The odds of that occurring increase with both a more complex uniform (i.e., those with a lot of parts, such as Full Dress) and when uniforms are packed for travel, rather than worn to the event.

The common omissions are items such as sporran, hose, flashes, caps, and waist belts; and, for "military" type uniforms, spats, and cross belts. However, and like other bands, we had omissions of greater concerns.

I recall one event at the Oregon coast, for which Full Dress was called as the uniform. When everyone arrived, one of the pipers realized he'd left his entire uniform at home, packed in a travel bag. He immediately blamed his wife for not collecting and bringing it. Nobody else bought his excuse; nor blamed his wife. And there certainly was nothing to be done; unless he wanted to drive back to his home in Washington State…a good two and a half hours each way.

Another omission was nearly as disastrous, though the member lucked out. We were attending a Tartan Ball in

Puyallup, Washington, put on by our friends in a Tacoma-based band, Clan Gordon. We were one of two guest pipe bands; and one of our pipers showed up with all…but his kilt. We found it rather amusing that he had every other part, except for one of the most important. Then again, we were not amused that we would be short one piper for our performance.

Fortunately, the other guest band was Washington Scottish. And that band wore the same tartan as our pipers: Royal Stewart. We were due to be the first guest band performing, and one of Washington Scottish's members was kind enough to loan his kilt to our member. We were thus able to go on with our routine with all pipers.

Sometimes, it was not a uniform omission; rather the wrong uniform. We had more than one event where a member showed up, for instance, in Full Dress, when Civilian was called. And even more common was someone with a mixture, such as all Civilian, except for a horsehair sporran (which is for military dress in our band; civilian being a round leather sporran).

At other times, the issue was more akin to uniform abuse. In traveling to events, many of us would carpool. And my most frequent band members with whom I traveled and stayed were Bill and Allan. Bill was always respectful with his uniform; Allan was far from it. I recall showing up at some event with Allan. I was already dressed, which is what I preferred to do. Allan did not; and when we arrived in the parking lot, he opened the trunk of his car. I looked in, and every uniform and all the parts were heaped inside. He reached in and pulled out a wrinkled tunic from the middle of his spare tire, asking, "Is this the right uniform?"

Then again, uniform issues were not always the problem. At

a Burns dinner in Portland, a tenor drummer showed up properly dressed, but realized she'd left her drum sitting on the floor of her living room.

THE BRASSIERE SOLOS

For many years, the Clan Band performed in the Oregon coastal town of Garibaldi. By "performed," I mean that we would march in a parade of just a few blocks, then start playing in pubs from north to south in the town, including "The Marina," "The Main Deck," "Ghost Hole," and ending at "Bozzio's." As we headed south through the town, the crowd accompanying us would grow; and by the time we reached Bozzio's, there was hardly any standing room.

In that pub, as in the others, we were treated with beer. In addition, the owner of Bozzio's would send around a tray of peppermint schnapps in shot glasses. Most people don't associate Scotsmen with schnapps; but we didn't argue, and continued to play. It was a rather rousing annual event, as you can well imagine.

One year, while playing, we saw a brassiere fly across the room. It landed right on the head of the Drum Sergeant, Ron, who kept on playing, the bra draped perfectly with the cups on either side of his head. The rest of us cracked up and stopped playing; but Ron continued on with a drum solo. Ron then stopped, took the bra and draped it over the head of the piper next to him and said, "Now you have to play a solo and pass it on." The piper did, then moved the bra to the next piper and around the circle, each playing a little solo with the bra draped on his head.

We finally asked, "Who threw that?" A young lady, perhaps in her thirties, said, "I did," and lifted her top to show she was, indeed, sans bra. An older lady next to her, looked shocked and said, "Oh, my God; that's my daughter!"

Post-Script: The next year, we again did the parade and usual "pub crawl" performance. As before, another brassiere, much larger, came flying across the room. I guess some in the crowd remembered the year before and decided upon a tradition. However, sometime after the parade, Bozzio's burned down. Also, the parade organizers indicated that there was no money to hire the band for their parade. So, sadly, our band has never returned to Garibaldi.

THE NIGHT BEACH GIG FROM A STORY TOLD BY JOE HEWITT AND BONNIE MACKENZIE

Sometime in the 1970s, the Clan Band was hired by a company to play for an evening beach party. I believe it was on the beach near Gearhart, which is on the Oregon coast between Seaside and Astoria.

As Joe described it, the party was at a beach bonfire and barbecue for corporate executives. The band was hired by one of the executives as a surprise for his colleagues. Consequently, the idea was for the band to march up the beach as close to the water as possible, then march over the dunes, emerging from the darkness to the more sheltered gathering as the surprise. What was not anticipated were near gale force winds!

As arranged, the band gathered in Full Dress uniform some distance south of the beach party and on the seaward side of the dunes. The band also had dancers accompanying it. The band struck up a tune and headed north up the beach. It was dark and difficult to see, for there were no lights beyond the ambient light from the town some distance over the dunes.

To make matters worse, the wind began rising significantly, and sand and saltwater started slamming into the band members from the side. Bonnie stated that she could see, on occasion, a band member or dancer nearly disappear in a hole in the sand, then popping back up. But the band played and marched on, yet with heads and bodies leaning more and more forward to counter what was beginning to be a gale. As they followed the Drum Major, Geordie Paterson, it was getting more difficult to see him through the darkness, wind and sand; and he appeared to be pulling ahead. Before long, the pipers and drummers lost sight of Geordie.

The band played on bravely, leaning into the wind. As Joe described it, "The sound just blew away and down the beach. All we could hear was a whining sound mixed with the wind." And having lost their D/M, the members didn't know where they were. The Pipe Major, however, finally noticed some light to the right over the dunes, hoping it was from the bonfire of the party. He veered the band in that direction, trudging through the deep sand of the dunes.

Switching perspective to that of the members of the beach party, they were apparently having a very good time. They were now quite lubricated and standing around the bonfire with drinks in hand. Imagine the surprise of seeing a lone figure emerging from the darkness of the beach, dressed in Full Highland Dress, with feather bonnet and mace. That was Drum Major Paterson.

Returning to the band's viewpoint, they finally made it over the dunes, playing and trudging from fatigue through the sand and wind. They observed their D/M, holding a beer and looking back at the band, along with a silent group of inebriated executives. But they'd arrived at the right spot and continued playing, as hired to do.

When they finished their tune, Joe said that the only sound was the wind. But then one of the executives broke the silence, saying, "Drinks?" There was no argument, and the band members enjoyed the next couple hours of drinking and warming up around the fire.

Post-Script: For many years, the Clan Band would hold its own beach barbecues, following the Garibaldi Parade and pub crawl. Nobody can recall anyone emerging from the darkness, or any other surprises.

"PACHELBEL'S CANON"

Sometime in the early 1990s, I believe, one of our long-time members, sometime Business Manager, and a very bright and funny attorney, John W. Osburn, approached me with something he'd scored for bagpipes: "Pachelbel's Canon in D Major." Not only had he scored it, but wrote it in three parts (i.e., melody and two harmony parts). It was an aggressive and impressive work; and John was justifiably proud of it, hoping that we would learn it.

Given John's long service, how highly he was regarded, and in considering all the work he'd put into it, we could not refuse. It was also very beautiful. And, in fact, there was a perfect event coming up at which it could be debuted: A Tattoo, put on in Salem by the then Oregon National Guard

Pipe Band. So we got to work on memorizing it. We decided, given the "Canon's" quiet sound, it did not need a drum score developed.

The evening of the event arrived, held at the Armory in Salem, Oregon, and there was quite a crowd in the sort of amphitheater seats. We were one of two guest pipe bands invited to perform, and our turn came. We entered on a couple marches, played some dance tunes, and then paused to debut John's rendition of "Pachelbel's Canon." With melody and two harmonies, it was complicated; but we felt that it came off well. And John was happy. We then finished up with some quick marches, leaving the floor.

After the event, we had a number of audience members approaching us to compliment the band on its performance. At one point, an elderly lady approached me. She said that she enjoyed our performance and thanked us for appearing. I smiled and thanked her. Then she said, "May I ask a question?" to which, still smiling, I said, "Of course." She said, "Why, in the middle of your program, did your band decide to retune your pipes?" It took me a few seconds to realize that was how she heard and interpreted "Pachelbel's Canon!"

AWKWAAAARD!: *FROM THE AUTHOR'S PERSONAL EXPERIENCE PLUS OTHERS' STORIES*

While I was a piping student, not quite ready to play pipes with the band, I was on tenor drum. One evening on St. Patrick's Day, we were playing out on the sidewalk in downtown Portland, Oregon, in front of McCormick & Schmick's restaurant/bar. A crowd was gathered around us, yet some traffic was also passing by, trying to avoid hitting revelers. I was twirling the sticks (mallets) when a string on one of them broke. The mallet flew through the air and landed on the roof of a passing car. While I stood in a bit of shock, a very inebriated spectator said, with considerably slurred speech, "I'll get it!" We continued to play, me with one mallet. Ten minutes later, the sweating, but smiling, retriever, came up to me and handed my mallet back. I smiled and thanked him, but there would be no more twirling with that mallet; and I couldn't play the drum, for it was an old rope tension drum with a head that was no more resonant than cardboard.

Ray was a Pipe Major of the band (1964-1972); and I was told this story about him at a wedding where he was hired to play. Band members, who would be playing at the reception, were at the wedding to observe as Ray started marching down the aisle, playing the bride in. He was clearly not regimental (also referred to as "commando" when sans underwear), for observers noticed some fabric emerging from underneath his kilt as he started down the aisle, leading in the bride. Boxer underwear continued creeping down as Ray continued marching and playing. Without any interruption, the underwear came down around his knees, at which point, Ray was able to kick them down and step out of them, never missing a beat, continuing down to the altar.

ROSE FESTIVAL TALES

As stated earlier, the Clan Band had played in most of Portland's Grand Floral Parade, commonly referred to as the "Rose Parade," and may play in future ones. It also played for a number of years in another Rose Festival event, the Starlight Parade (a shorter, evening parade that occurs a week before the Grand Floral Parade). With that history in mind, there are many stories accompanying the band's participation in both. These are just a few:

Atrophy in Whites. The Rose Parade occurs early in June; and the weather in Oregon is unpredictable at that time. It can be cool and rainy, or it can be hot as dickens…or somewhere in between. It's staggering to realize that our band often did that parade in Full Dress, with feather bonnets. When I was P/M, I called for the cooler summer military. Even if we were chilly in the morning, we would certainly warm up during what is a very long parade (over 5 miles). But one year, we had new white tunics (thanks to Bill Furman of Greenbrier); and we decided to sport them. They were good looking, and we felt they would be cool enough on what turned out to be one of the warmer parades. So we thought!

The parade started as usual, with us marching through the old Coliseum, filled with a crowd, then emerging to another crowd and past the initial cameras and TV announcers, then turning onto the first of many streets. It was bright and warm; and, as usual, whenever we stopped between tunes, many in the crowd would yell, "Play!" It's why, much to the dismay of our band, I called tunes frequently, with little break between. We were, after all, there for the crowd. However, on this parade the weather was getting warmer and, with stalls in the parade (leaving us standing in the sun), along with the playing, some of our members began to struggle. The dress whites, it turned out, weren't that cool; and the temperature had risen to the 90s.

Halfway in, a drummer dropped out; then another. In another

mile, a piper stepped out and said, "I'll meet you at the pub." Another drummer and piper followed. In addition, pipers were getting blown out (meaning they just couldn't keep the pipes going), and the remaining drummers were struggling to keep up. By the time we reached the uphill climb of the last leg (going past the county library), we had perhaps three pipers still playing out of the ten or twelve "survivors." We braved it to the end, where some welcome water awaited us. We recovered enough to get real refreshment at the nearest pub!

Uphill Hornpipe. Speaking of that uphill climb past the library, one year I called a hornpipe at that point in the parade. I believe it was "The Jolly Beggarman." I don't know why, but I knew we were near the end, and I thought we'd play something "catchy" and strut-worthy for the crowd. I'm not certain why band members felt it was cruel to play something fast—at least for the fingers—on the uphill, but some clearly did. For no sooner had I called it off, that I heard some moans. Then, after we played it, I heard from the rear, "Hubbard, you asshole!" I thought that was pretty funny, and ever since then, whenever we had a parade, I would call a hornpipe on any uphill portion! It even reached a point where, in certain parades, some members would call out, "We have an uphill coming!"

The Great Choke. The Clan Band always had a reputation of putting things together, sometimes at the last moment. The band was always very flexible, no matter what impediments were in the way or changes in any routine developed. But there was one particular event, during the Starlight Parade, which was rather embarrassing. As mentioned before, the

Starlight Parade is an evening parade the week before the Rose Parade.

To set the stage, there are some tunes that can be more difficult from a memory standpoint. Sometimes, a tune, for whatever reason, is difficult to remember how it starts again when played "time about" (meaning repeated). For us, "Peter MacKenzie Warren" was one of those tunes.

So we had reached a point in the parade where TV commentators were stationed and there were huge lights overlooking each parade entrant. Our P/M at the time stopped us before the lights. In the meantime, the commentators (we watched the rerun of the parade afterward) were talking about the band, the uniforms, etc. And one said, "This is my favorite band." Well, the P/M had called the dreaded "Peter MacKenzie Warren," and we'd started marching toward the lights and cameras as the commentators were talking about the band.

Just when the commentator said, "Let's listen," the tune was about to begin again…and we had a massive choke. In other words, everyone stopped to listen to their neighbor piper on how the tune started again! Everyone! So there was dead silence; then a few squeaks as a few attempted to remember the tune and start up. It didn't work, and everyone gave up and the band continued marching with no sound. The commentators were silent, too; but then went on to describe the float that followed. We resumed after we'd passed the cameras and finished the parade, knowing we'd mull this over at the next practice. In fact, I believe we never did the Starlight Parade again.

The Burning Float. In the Rose Parade, we were behind a float (I don't recall of what, though I recall that it was somewhat enclosed, like a house). We were on the Burnside Bridge when we noticed some green liquid running out underneath the float (I assume it was radiator fluid). Then we saw smoke, and some individuals jumping out of the float. We were stopped, but our D/M, Geordie Paterson, started us up quickly and we marched around the float, through developing smoke, before flames started. We got around it; and, as far as we know, the rest of the parade behind us was trapped for some time. A number of spectators along the rest of the parade route thought that we were the end of the parade.

A Parade's Pace. We have always thought that a bagpipe band should lead a parade, if for no other reason than to establish a sensible pace. But that advice is never taken; perhaps (we'd like to think) because parade organizers like to save the best for later. In any event, many parades end up being like accordions, starting, stopping, starting, spreading out, crushing together, and so on. In the Rose Parade, that often happened when large floats were navigating corners…or when something happened (like a burning float!).

One year, however, the pace was rapid, and as fast as we were marching, a huge gap developed between the float ahead of us and our band. Some parade stewards came up and said, "Speed it up." One piper yelled out, "A pipe band doesn't move as fast as a Buick!" But they did not care, and repeated that we needed to speed up. We did quicken our pace. However, when our P/M called off a tune, there was no roll-off from the drum corps. He called it off again, but nothing. We finally looked back, and realized we'd left the drum corps two blocks back. Carrying drums limits one's marching speed, and we'd left them in the dust, all the time hearing spectators yelling, "Play!" Afterward, we told the Committee that we would not do the parade again if that's the pace they expected. They never bothered us after that.

On a related note of gaps in a parade, one year it had nothing to do with our pace. We had a dance/singing group ahead of us (why would anyone put another musical group near a pipe band? But that's another topic). As we emerged from the Coliseum to march while playing before the cameras and commentators, we were signaled to stop. The musical song and dance group was performing for the cameras, while the parade ahead of them continued on. The group finished a tune, and we got ready to continue. But no! They started up another routine. We looked at each other, all thinking *What the hell!* for we were watching the preceding parade disappear. By the time they were done, and we were signaled to proceed, there must have been a half mile gap between the parade ahead and the song and dance group. For the rest of the parade, we were observing spectators wandering about, wondering if there was still a parade. Fortunately, nobody asked us or the preceding group to speed up.

BAD UNIFORM CALL

For most events, the P/M calls the uniform, although with input from others, especially the D/M. Factors that influence that call involve the setting, type of event, weather conditions (when outside), and other factors. The band currently has three basic uniforms, although it's had a fourth. The three are Full Dress (with variations, such as type of cap), Summer Military, and Civilian. The fourth, if utilized, is Full Dress Whites.

For outdoor events when it's cold, such as a January barge

launch, Full Dress, due to the wool tunics, etc., is welcome. Full Dress is also often called for very formal and "showy" events, such as the Clan Gordon Tartan Ball, for it's a crowd pleaser. For summer parades, we usually sport the Summer Military, for it's the coolest of the uniforms. For competition, we wear Civilian, as do most competition bands.

One year, we were invited to play a parade in Tillamook, Oregon. I believe it was a 4th of July parade. Tillamook is a coastal city; and in summers, when it may be warm inland, the coast often has a cool, misty climate. Believing that to be the case, I called for Full Dress, with feather bonnets. Well, that was a bad call! We arrived to a sunny day and 86 degrees. Most unusual for the coast; and most unfortunate to us! And, of course, I heard about it from our members!

We started playing and marching; and when we turned the corner to the main street, three senses and one thought hit me. The senses were the visual one of a sea of nearly naked bodies; the overwhelming smell of coconut oil; and hearing a large "Whoa" from the crowd…I guess in disbelief that anyone would show up on a hot day in such a uniform. The thought I had was, "Oh, no! I'll end up killing old Fraser!" We had a piper in the ranks who was in his eighties, and I was not sure he would last, let alone survive. He did, however. And we were able to laugh over it when we made it to an air conditioned pub and cold beer.

DANCE FOIBLES

The Sword Dance Competition. From around 1978/79 until the mid-1980s, the band had a couple of dance routines as part of some performances. The first was a four-man sword dance (we had no women in the band back then). A number of us took lessons from Bonnie MacKenzie of the MacKenzie Dance Company. During some band performances, four members would have dancing ghillies on. At some point, instruments would be set down by them and they would put crossed swords in the middle of a circle the band made. The band would strike in, and the four would dance around the swords. Even though we weren't the most talented dancers, it was a crowd pleaser.

After having taken lessons and performed for a few years, Bonnie suggested that we compete. So two of us entered the sword dance competition at the Portland Highland Games; the others chickened out! In any event, at those games, I found myself on a wood platform, with one of our other members, Bill—a much better dancer (and piper) than I—to my right. To my left were two or three young ladies in an upper grade (so in this round, I was just competing with Bill). The dance piper started, we did our bow, and started to dance around and between the crossed swords in front of each of us. Amongst other factors being graded was that we never touch the swords.

I was concentrating as best I could; yet about half way through, a sword came zinging past me from my right. I could hear Bill saying, "Oh, no! Oh, no!" I wanted to laugh, but I knew I would blow my routine. Mercifully, I got through it, knowing that I had likely beat Bill (though I felt bad for him, and wouldn't otherwise deserve it).

Well, a few minutes later, a steward came and explained that the piper stopped short (for the young ladies on the platform) and that we had to do it all over again. I was deflated, having made it through a competition; but Bill was happy to get another opportunity. So we got on the platform and started it all over. Well, about half way through…another sword came zinging past me from my right! I couldn't believe it; and it was all I could do to get through the competition without my own foible. I ended up taking 3rd, clearly by default. I don't know who took the first two spots. It was probably some youngsters.

Swan Song. After doing the sword dance routine for some time, Bonnie choreographed another dance, "Wilt Though Go to Barracks, Johnny," for three of us. It ended up being the last dance we would do, and it premiered (and ended) at an evening event we did near the Rose Garden in Portland, called "A Highland Evening". At some point, David, Allan and I stepped out from the band and walked up on stage. The band started playing, and the dance was supposed to have us, in unison, moving back and forth, right to left, back and forth. Well, it started out OK. But at some point, Allan and I (who was in the middle) moved back to the right; but David moved left. He and I collided, and the audience started laughing. We never recovered, for each time we started moving, David and I were always going opposite. We must have collided four or more times. As I said, we danced no more, though we were unintentionally entertaining!

Part Four:
PHOTOGRAPHS, MUSIC, AND MISCELLANOUS

THERE IS NO WAY to provide all the photographs ever taken of the Clan Band, its members, activities, and so forth. In addition to what has already been shared, we're including on the following pages a number of photos to represent the band through the decades.

In addition, there have been Clan Band-related tunes written, as well as tunes written by members. We're sharing some of those, as well (and for which permission has been given, when needed).

CLAN BAND

Early photo of the band in Dress Whites. Perhaps early 1930s. Note all the medals!

Band at the Clan Gordon Tartan Ball, Puyallup, Washington, 2019. *L to R*: Bob Thuemmel, P/M Tomas Peralta, P/S Jeff Robins, P/S Michael Hubbard, Jayne Ferlitsch, Alex Smith, Dan Dorsett, D/M Linda Mae Dennis, Katie Nordone, Karen Woodall, D/S Bill Duncan, Joyce Dorsett, Pete Woodall, Skip Adams, Kathleen O'Brian.

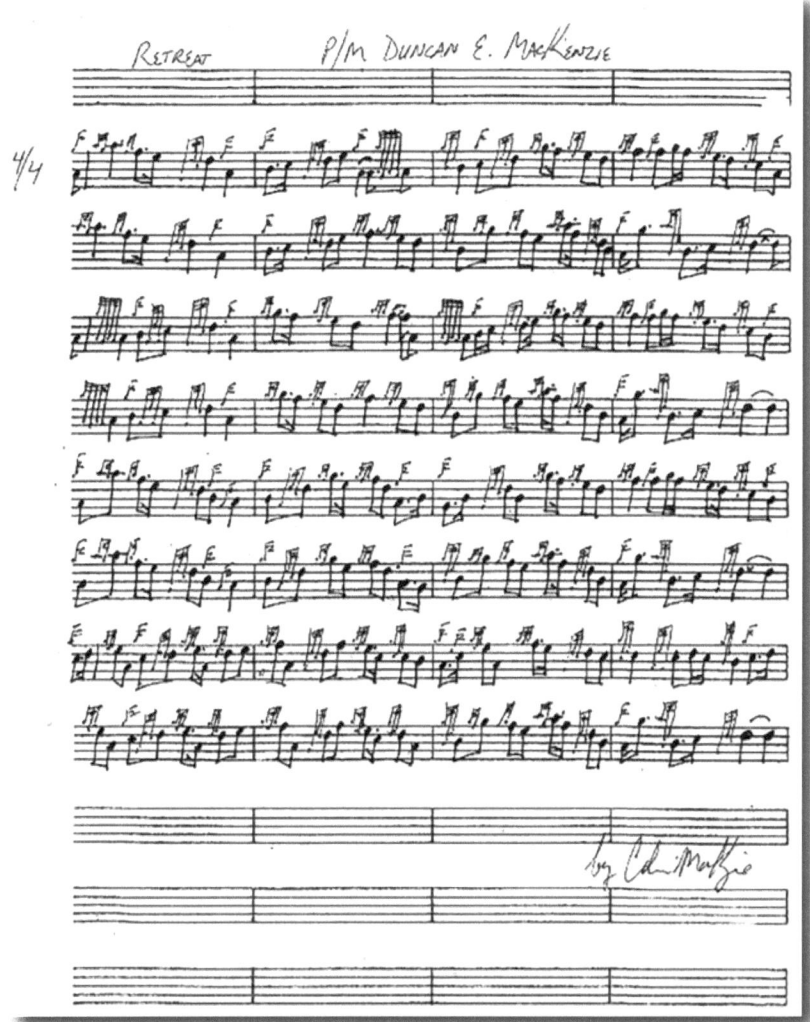

An original composition by Colin MacKenzie written for his father, Duncan, on his 80th birthday in 1997.

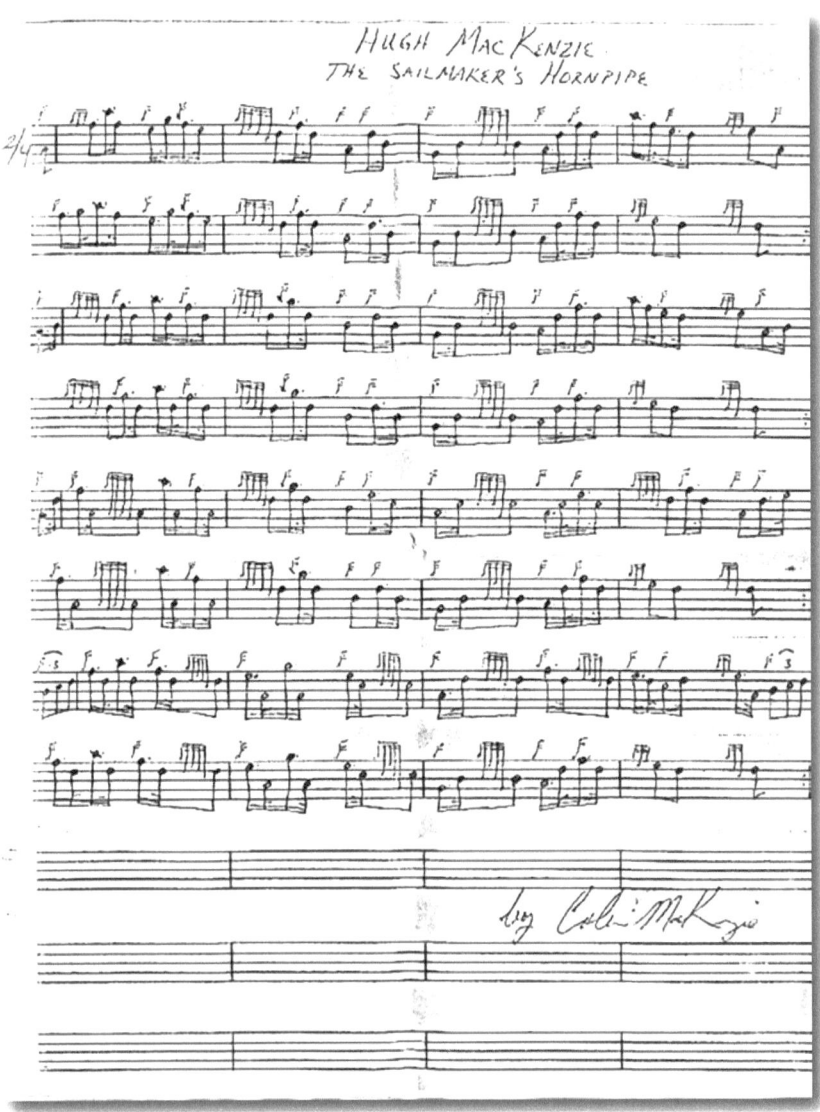

Another original composition by Colin MacKenzie written for his father, Duncan. This one was for Duncan's 83rd birthday in 2004.

Playing at opening ceremony of the Portland Highland Games, July 2012. It was around 100 degrees F.

CLAN BAND

Written as a tribute from the Clan Band to Gunderson/Greenbrier, which has hired the band for barge launches and other events for the past twenty-five plus years.

Barge Launch. March 2014. Photo taken from top of barge by one of the soloists. In the earlier days of the launches, a piper would volunteer to be on the barge to play the first part of "Amazing Grace," with the band joining in the second time through. This would typically follow a prayer given by one of the guest ministers or priests. The solo piper, however, was then part of those riding the barge into the water. Often, the band would then play at a Gunderson-hosted brunch or luncheon for the Gunderson's guests and other VIPs; and the solo piper would often be stuck on the barge until it was pushed back for disembarking.

Drum corps having fun, circa 1987. D/M George Paterson, Ron Galloway, David Day, Joe Hewitt. Pipe Sergeant Bill Farr is in the background.

Two Clan Band Pipe Majors in the beer garden at Portland Highland Games. 1990. L to R: Michael Hubbard (P/M 1988-1994 and 1998-2017) and Jeff Brewer (P/M 1980-1988).

A very creative photo by Harold Hutchinson at the Gunderson Family Picnic. Alderbrook Park, Washington, 2014. The band was actually situated in a concave curve, but the panoramic photo came out convex to show everyone better.

Clan Band and dancers at opening ceremony of Portland Highland Games at Jantzen Beach, Oregon, 1952.

Fourth of July Parade, Salem, Oregon, circa 1950s.

Following the Miracle Mile Parade, 1956.

Another 1956 gathering with dancers, a practice that was common for decades.

Clan Macleay at the Tartan Ball in 1957.

Massed Bands at Tartan Ball in 2005.

Piping at a movie premiere, 1958.

Formal shot of band at Pittock Mansion, Portland, Oregon, circa 2007.

Grand Floral (Rose) Parade, 1989. P/M Michael Hubbard, Don Stewart, and Joe Chartier. Photo from *The Oregonian*.

CLAN BAND

Gathering of Grand Floral (Rose) Parade Participants, 1961.

In 2019, the Clan Band was honored to have its D/M Dan Kelley (in troos) at the Edinburgh Tattoo.

For many years, the band had an annual barbecue at Pat Sheaffer's home, usually with a lamb roasted by Tom Lekas. Here, Jeff Brewer is piping in the lamb, carried by Tom (in apron), circa 1980.

George Paterson (at microphone) with Miss Oregon at Clan Macleay Tartan Ball, 1957.

CLAN BAND

Bonnie Heather Blyth with P/M Duncan MacKenzie. Bonnie would marry Colin MacKenzie, Duncan's son, and they would have two daughters, Holly and Shona. Bonnie owned the Bonnie MacKenzie Dance Company and produced many outstanding dancers and instructors.

A young Colin MacKenzie performing the sword dance.

CLAN BAND

Portland Highland Games, with D/M George Paterson and P/M Jack Taylor, circa 1979.

Joe Chartier, John Waddingham, Lynn Easton, and James Wallace.

Clan Band circa the 1930s.

Mini-band at a Gunderson event in 2017. *Front*: P/M Michael Hubbard and future P/M Tomas Peralta. *Back*: Kevin Kelley (on bass), Bob Thuemmel, Troy Jesse, Karen Woodall and Pete Woodall.

Joe Hewitt and Bill Farr.

Drum Major George Paterson, circa 2010.

Pipe Major Michael Hubbard and D/M George Paterson at Gunderson Barge Launch, 2005.

Clan Tent at Athena Games, Athena, Oregon, 2018. *L to R*: Mylinda Fletcher Humble, Alex Smith, Karen Woodall, P/M Tomas Peralta, Pete Woodall, and Linda Mae Dennis.

Marching into competition at Tacoma Highland Games, 2007.

Circled up for competition at Portland Highland Games, playing Grade 4 medley, 2007.

In the beer garden at Skagit Valley Highland Games, Mt. Vernon, Washington. *L to R*: Greg Dinse, P/M Michael Hubbard, Scott Henderson, and Brian MacKenzie.

At The Dock Pub in New Glasgow, Nova Scotia, 1996. P/M David Bueermann, Dan Kelley, Michael Hubbard.

At Willamette University, Salem, Oregon, 2019. *L to R*: Mylinda Fletcher Humble, Michael Hubbard, P/M Tomas Peralta, John Goff, D/S Bill Duncan, and Kevin Kelley. We played for three different commencements.

CLAN BAND

At Cornelius Pass Roadhouse after Hillsboro 4th of July Parade. *L to R*: Dan Kelley, Bill Farr, John W. Osburn, George Paterson. Down in the corner is Mark Cameron.

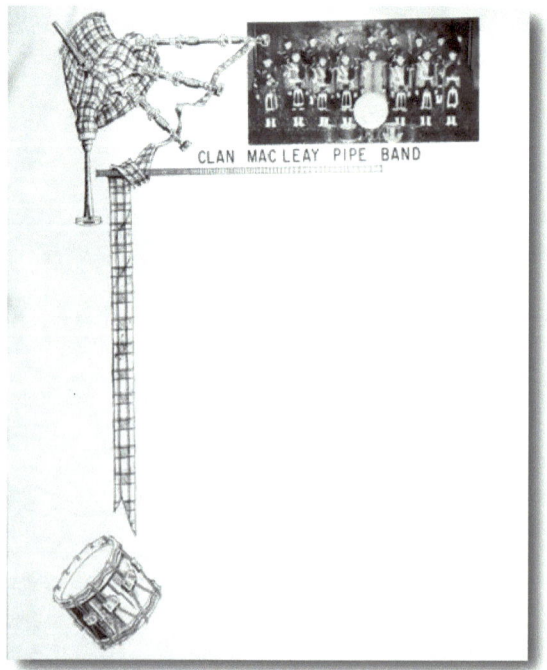

Clan Macleay Pipe Band stationery, circa 1954.

The Clan Band cover and article featured in a local weekly magazine, 1989.

"Mad Dog" Cooper! Howard Cooper was my first instructor. Far from the truth about this kind gentleman and Pipe Sergeant, which is what made the moniker so funny to us all.

ACKNOWLEDGMENTS

This work would not be possible without the assistance and support from so many, past and present; in fact, too many to thank enough. For those no longer with us, my appreciation goes to our longtime friend, Joe Hewitt; as well as to Bob Johnson; Harry Fenley; Duncan MacKenzie; and my original instructor, Howard Cooper.

So many others have assisted in various ways. They include another longtime friend and bandmate, Dr. William Farr, our band's Pipe Sergeant and secretary/treasurer, who assisted with access to the Oregon Historical Society and research, and encouraged me; Margaret (Farr) Nickerson, who supplied so many vintage photographs and other information. Thanks also to Tomas Peralta; Pat Peralta; Skip Adams; Julie Ward; Bill Furman; Maureen Winney; Mylinda Fletcher Humble; Jeff Robins; Katie Nordone; Allan Muir; and Brad Collins—all for assistance, submissions and encouragement.

Much of this work would not be complete without special help from the MacKenzie family and relatives, including Colin MacKenzie, Bonnie Heather Blyth MacKenzie, Marianna MacKenzie Day, Shona MacKenzie, and David Day. Also, my brother, Kim, provided most excellent editing and suggestions.

Thanks also to the Oregon Historical Society; Multnomah County Library; *The Oregonian*; Andrew Lenz; my brother,

Mitch; Uncle Bob and Aunt Cathie Favret; and, of course, my wife, Beth Doyle.

To all others I've not mentioned, my apologies, yet my gratitude.

ABOUT THE AUTHOR

PHOTO BY KEN MACKENZIE.

MICHAEL C. HUBBARD IS a retired mental health therapist, with prior careers in medicine, biotechnology and business. Mr. Hubbard has been a bagpiper and instructor for forty years, and has played with several bands, yet always with the Clan Macleay Pipe Band of Portland, Oregon, of which he was Pipe Major for nearly twenty-five years. He and his wife, Beth, live on their farm in Oregon.

www.hellgatepress.com

www.ingramcontent.com/pod-product-compliance
Lightning Source LLC
Chambersburg PA
CBHW042314150426
43201CB00001B/1